climbing gardens

climbing gardens

adding height and structure to your garden

JOAN CLIFTON

SPECIAL PHOTOGRAPHY BY STEVEN WOOSTER

FRANCES LINCOLN

for my mother – thank you for enabling me to see the unexpected

CLIMBING GARDENS

Frances Lincoln Limited
4 Torriano Mews
Torriano Avenue
London NW5 2RZ

First Frances Lincoln Edition: 2001

British Library Cataloguing-in-Publication Data
A catalogue record for this book is available from the British Library

ISBN 0-7112-1607-X

Printed in Singapore

9 8 7 6 5 4 3 2 1

page 1 Curling tendrils and twining stems inspired the design of this spiralling
wirework plant trainer, here being taken advantage of by the sinuous progress of a
precocious pink sweet pea.

pages 2 and 3 Climbing structures enable you to create potent architectural
statements in garden design. The view through (**left**) and towards (**right**) a window
cut into a tall hornbeam hedge looks along a romantic pergola composed of a series
of rectangular frames. Diamond-pattern trelliswork facings have been used to
lighten the visual effect of the substantial structure, while the generous proportions
and powerful horizontals and verticals reflect the bold planting of wisteria, roses,
honeysuckle and clematis.

opposite and above How could we ever presume to
supersede the design capabilities of the natural world?
The passionflower, though growing from roots in the
ground, seems to suggest a strange sea creature with
waving tentacles and built-in propellers and navigation
equipment, while its tendrils form perfect spirals.
Deceptively innocent in virginal white, *Passiflora caerulea*
'Constance Elliot' makes a definitive case for the
cultivation of the greatest number of fine climbing plants
that can be coaxed up an edifice in your garden.

CONTENTS

introduction

If you think of a garden simply as a flat surface out of which plants grow, you are missing the point! A garden should be a three-dimensional space, filled with colour, texture and dynamic form, which you can walk through, look at and feel.

It is the vertical dimension that transforms it from a flat palette into a theatrical experience that gives you new vistas and views at every turn. For your garden to be a living, year-round production that will reward you with changing scenes throughout the cycle of seasons, the vertical elements are as essential as the backdrop, scenery and props of any stage.

It is of course perfectly possible to create an interesting three-dimensional space with planting alone – by selecting trees and shrubs of differing shapes, heights, growth rates and seasonal qualities. However, the addition of man-made vertical features allows a more flexible, holistic approach to garden design. Such features create an instant sense of scale, and provide permanent, all-seasons structure and pleasing contrasts of texture. They are particularly valuable when creating a new garden, providing decorative height and structure even before they are clothed with plants. Large expanses can be pulled into focus and articulated by tall trees and hedges, but these take a considerable time to establish themselves and by nature offer limited design options. On the other hand, a pergola, for example, can define spatial division either lightly through delicate architectural metalwork, or more robustly with sturdy timbers draped with sumptuous displays of flowering plants. Clever use

Bravely formal in a rural landscape, these bold wooden obelisks introduce a three-dimensional definition to the otherwise informal planting in a pair of borders. The simplicity of their design dynamically imposes order and belies the complexity of the role they play—they are temporarily supporting rambling roses while they form the shapes of nascent yew topiary.

of structures like *trompe l'oeil* treillage can make small gardens appear larger, and decorative screens can disguise ugly walls or fences or bring shelter and privacy, as well as interest, to crowded urban spaces and roof terraces.

Vertical structures make some of the most valuable eye-catching focal points, especially when balanced by sympathetic and appropriate planting. Imagine a secluded seating arbour veiled by clouds of scented jasmine, or a pair of neatly trimmed ivy-covered obelisks framing and emphasizing the formality of an entrance. Vertical features can also bring a sense of order to an otherwise haphazard planting scheme: think of a row of rose-wreathed pillars rising from an unruly herbaceous border.

Plants can themselves make living vertical statements. However, it is only those that depend upon an underlying permanent structure and the hand of man in pruning and training that are candidates for this book. Think of willow woven into fences and arbours; yew, hornbeam and beech clipped into aerial screens; or plants trained to fill out wirework frames that range from geometric cones to fanciful armchairs.

Vertical elements have played a key decorative role in gardens since the Classical era. We know, from excavated mosaics and wall paintings, that the Romans dined beneath pergolas and enclosed their gardens with trelliswork fences. In the fifteenth century, from when detailed visual evidence survives, tunnel arbours – or pergolas – abounded, elaborate latticework was used to make enclosures and screens of all kinds, and trees and shrubs were trained into elaborate shapes. By the seventeenth century, books were being published with designs for carpentry-work obelisks and gazebos. Today, now that the constraints of twenty-first-century living are resulting in smaller gardens, leaving many of us with diminutive and preciously guarded outdoor spaces, the potential of the vertical dimension is more important than ever. Gardeners need to make the most of that dimension in order to use every iota of valuable space.

The choice of structures and materials for vertical features has never been wider than it is today. As well as being available in conventional forms made of traditional materials, such as wrought iron and timber, structures are being made in new designs fashioned in materials such as steel and nylon that were formerly associated with industry. These structures are delicate in appearance and yet have the necessary strength to support exuberant growth. Whether you make use of readily available, off-the-shelf structures, opt for specially commissioned designs, or invent them yourself, there is a range of possibilities to suit every

requirement and taste, from serenely formal to overtly romantic to minimally urban.

For the gardener who is as interested in plants as in spatial design, these structures provide perfect excuses to grow more and more climbers. When choosing plants for vertical features, it is important to understand each plant's method of attachment before selecting it for a specific purpose. For example, the vigorous Virginia creeper (*Parthenocissus quinquefolia*) is self-clinging, attaching itself by suckers, so it requires a solid and expansive surface like a wall upon which to hoist itself, and will not thank you for giving it a fine wirework obelisk for support. On the other hand, an obelisk is ideal for summer-flowering clematis, which attaches itself with curling tendrils and will be happy wrapping these tightly around the wire frame. The directory of plants on pages 112–141 explains the different ways in which plants clamber upwards, and suggests the most suitable types of support within each main entry. (The directory also specifies the zones in which the various plants are hardy.) Walls can make wonderful backdrops for almost any plants, but three-dimensional, open-framework constructions like pergolas and obelisks allow the astonishing qualities of stems and foliage to be seen better and the full beauty and grace of flowers to be shown off to their full advantage.

The chapters that follow have been divided to explore the possibilities of vertical structures and climbing plants according to the way that most people see their gardens – either as a vehicle for their chosen style, as an outdoor extension of their living space, or as a place to grow produce for the kitchen. But of course a single volume cannot hope to provide all the answers; rather, it should be treated as a starter pack. Use it to point you in a sympathetic direction and then let your imagination take off. If there is a message in this book, it is to let the freedom of outdoor space encourage you to take creative risks that would be unthinkable indoors.

The effervescent spirit of climbers is summed up by the scrambling habit of *Clematis montana*. The pure white simplicity of this single-flowered plant reflects the freshness of spring, when it will exuberantly smother a wall or arbour with delicately scented blooms.

Planting structures are the tools with which you can develop the decorative potential as well as the vertical dimensions of a garden. Used with imagination, they can turn functional needs into visual advantages, transforming the appearance of a garden at the same time as extending its physical scope. In the form of two-dimensional screening or three-dimensional constructions, or as freestanding eye-catchers, they play a crucial role in the overall design of the space, contributing architectural interest and personal style.

On this imposing estate, an appropriately dignified, open-latticed screen has been formed from a series of arching sections. A clear aperture pierces its progression, providing both a vista and access to the house beyond. Masses of luxuriant *Rosa* 'Paul's Scarlet Climber' romantically foil the otherwise taut formality of the wrought-iron structure.

STRUCTURES

Vertical elements reinforce the underlying structure of a garden design. They play a crucial role in overall shape and form by creating architectural interest with enclosure, divisions and varying heights, and with punctuation and focal points. And, as well as giving visual interest throughout the year, they offer support for a myriad plants.

A fully developed garden design takes into account both spatial and functional considerations. A row of arches, for example, can turn a simple path linking a garage with the house into a romantic tunnel festooned with pale mauve racemes of wisteria, while a pair of brightly painted, clematis-covered obelisks can make a mundane border look spectacular. Even a single wire cone, hosting the extravagant azure trumpets of a morning glory, can transform the sense of space and style of a tiny back yard.

Most gardens need some form of enclosure to provide privacy or to block out a view, or division to demarcate and contain different areas of a garden. In a confined, urban space, where privacy is at a premium, enclosure becomes crucial. Whether you are trying to hide from neighbours or obscure an undesirable view, your first instincts may be to construct high, solid barriers. However, unless you have a large garden, these instincts are best suppressed, as the results can be claustrophobic in effect and also, more importantly, cut out the light and air that are essential to plant life. A more practical option is to raise the height of a wall or fence above eye level with a strong lattice screen. This will admit sunlight while diffusing the view and provide necessary support and air flow for a wide variety of climbing plants.

Particularly in small spaces, openwork screens are also an ideal means of dividing a garden into separate spaces. Creating distinctive areas, or 'rooms', can increase the apparent size of the overall space and also add a sense of mystery and discovery as you pass from one to another. It is wonderful to walk through a garden that reveals its qualities gradually. Encountering surprises or unexpected vistas gives me a delightful sense of exploration. Solid divisions make the sudden gaps between, and views through, them more exciting, but a screen that is not completely opaque combines the best of both worlds, giving firm boundaries as well as intriguing glimpses of what is to come.

Screening plays a key role as the permanent frame and backdrop of your garden, especially during the leafless winter months. The choice of material and style is almost limitless. Screens can be made of wood, metal, bamboo, rope or living willow, and may be fashioned in a style that will reflect your personal preferences and complement the architectural style of your home.

Timber is the most versatile and readily available material, as well as being generally the easiest to install. It is usually made into basic trellis panels, arranged in diamond or square patterns, but though common, these need never be run of the mill. Even the most basic trellis – or solid wooden fencing panels – can be jazzed up with an unusual colour of special exterior wood stain. More interesting off-the-shelf panels are becoming available in an ever-increasing number of designs – in swags and arches as well as rectangles, with a variety of decorative finials. You can combine these in different ways and personalize them with a colourful exterior timber finish, which can be coordinated with containers and outdoor furniture. I find that cool grey-greens and deep Mediterranean blues set off plants excellently, but there are no rules against using dazzling yellow, or searing red, if you can live with the effect. If you want a complex construction, especially one involving trompe l'oeil effects (see page 28), the detailing and finish of a specially commissioned scheme built by experts is generally most appropriate.

If you already have a solid, sturdy but dull fence, or an ugly wall or shed, panels of decorative timber trelliswork make excellent disguise. They can be easily attached, either to the existing uprights or to the wall, by bolts or screws or masonry pins. Keep the panels off the solid surface using blocks of timber as spacers, to allow the plants to twine and air to circulate. To prevent long-term maintenance problems, you can attach the panels with hinges at the base, and bolts or hooks and eyes at the top. This makes it possible to hinge the whole panel gently away from the solid backdrop just enough to repaint it if it becomes necessary.

If you want a more streamlined, less conventional effect than that given by trellising, you can make screening panels or fences of narrow, planed timber slats set vertically with small spaces

opposite Timber and brick are compatible materials that rarely fail to create pleasing partnerships with plants. Diamond trellis is light, airy and visually restful, but also totally efficient as a support with numerous anchor points for tying in climbing stems. Whether made from soft- or hardwood, it will last for many years if protected with a coat of paint or preservative. Here a fashionably distressed blue wood finish complements the soft greens and sunny yellow blooms of *Fremontodendron californicum*.

below Neat latticed fences enclosing this spacious waterside dining area work on two levels. As a design element, they echo the timber floor decking and provide formal definition to a private gathering place, but they also succeed in practical terms as solid supports for the roses and other climbers that soften the firm outline and link the space with the rest of the garden.

between them to admit light. When varnished a natural colour, these lend an urbane sophistication to a city garden. When painted, they could either complement a classical theme of greys and olives or make a funky, tropical clash of bright pink and orange.

Bamboo can be used to make screens that lend themselves to less traditional gardens, or to those with a calm, oriental feel. Available in many thicknesses, and also colours (the beauty of the black bamboo, *Phyllostachys nigra,* is its ebony-coloured stems), bamboo can be used cut to length as basic construction elements, or may be split for weaving into panels of varying density. Since poles crack easily when pierced with nails, joints are usually made by lashing the pieces together with sisal, rattan or coconut fibre string, or with split bamboo strips, about 2cm ($^3/_4$in) wide and only 2–5mm ($^1/_8$–$^1/_4$in) thick, shaved from poles with a sharp knife.

While timber can give a feeling of weight and substance, metals have special qualities that allow delicate visual effects while maintaining strength and durability. It is worth remembering that metal is a good conductor of temperature, and extremes of heat and cold can affect the plants – especially young shoots – with which it has direct contact. Iron can be hand-worked into geometric patterns or, for more classical settings, into screens combining twining and twisting shapes that suggest the forms of stems and leaves. Perhaps surprisingly, it is easier than many people think to commission special ironwork from a local blacksmith; if this appeals to you, make enquiries through your local business directory. Fine wirework, which can be hand woven into intricate designs normally associated with Victorian conservatories, can, with updated detailing, look just right for 'new romantic' gardens.

Industrial stainless steel and aluminium are now coming into their own for minimalist contemporary designs, for which a technical appearance would be appropriate. A wide variety of mesh forms, suitable to make up into panels, is obtainable at builder's merchants; alternatively, screens can be constructed from square or round tubing set vertically or horizontally between rails. Ordinary copper tubing, normally used for domestic plumbing, can also be hammered flat and welded into patterns.

Roof gardens and balconies, which require a combination of privacy from onlookers and shelter from sun and wind, also need barriers strong enough to prevent anyone from falling. In a contemporary design, the immensely strong, multi-stranded steel wiring used in yacht rigging can be given a new role, tensioned by using special bolts, and positioned in parallel rows between corner posts and walls to make light and sophisticated screening. Unlike many other metal structures, it is a relatively easy job to do yourself.

left above The rails of this bamboo screen are lashed to the vertical posts in authentic Japanese style, with split bamboo.

left below A simple but lovingly crafted ironwork fence animates a climbing rose with leaves, pigeons and smaller birds, all cut from thin but durable sheet metal.

right above The cool finish and uncluttered lines of stainless steel introduce a contemporary element that suits the simple monochrome texture of plain green ivy.

right below A colonnade of lattice pillars provides height and light enclosure on this rooftop garden. Their simple open structure, capped for stability and long life, offers elegant support for *Trachelospermum jasminoides*, which transforms them into a series of bold upright accents underplanted by seasonal bedding plants.

below In the early stages of creating a 'laid' hedge, young saplings have been cut three-quarters of the way through their trunks near the base and bent at an angle. They have been woven between evenly spaced stakes so that all the bushy ends project on the outside of the circle. The stakes, trimmed to a uniform height, are linked and reinforced at the top with a weft of tightly rolled binders of thin willow wands. Twiggy brushwood has been used as a temporary filler in the intervening spaces.

opposite A gap in a hedge has been transformed into an inspired 'eye' or *oeil de boeuf*. It frames the view to the fruit trees in the garden beyond to make a charming cameo and a window on to areas yet to be explored. Young green stems of willow and other sappy trees or shrubs are easily twisted, looped and secured with thinner twists of the same material, leaving both ends for weaving and fastening into the body of the hedge.

Rustic or organically styled gardens will benefit from screening of a less structured type. You can exploit the natural variations of colour and texture and the pliable habit of shrubs such as hazel, willow and bamboo to advantage by weaving or tying their stems together. The quick-rooting nature of willow even allows you to make living installations. By planting the pollarded whips in rows, and varying the angle and spacing, you can create bucolic boundaries and screens, forming lattices of diamonds or curving wavy patterns. In summer, the delicate foliage provides a graceful and natural hedge of pale green, narrow, rustling leaves. In winter, its deciduous character reveals a fine tracery of bare stems after leaf-drop. A varied selection of the many willow species in cultivation will result in a stunning cold-weather show that combines yellows and rusts, purples and blacks. You can vary the weaving in response to the required density. Closely set interweaving will result in opaque, leafy enclosures for privacy. Widely spaced stems that allow dappled sunlight to pass through make attractive open screening suitable for dividing up areas in a larger garden (see page 56).

More solid, but soft, living divisions can be made with traditional hedging. In larger gardens yew, beech and hornbeam can be pruned and trained to make interesting ornamental screens that are pierced with round or rectangular 'windows'. Hornbeam (*Carpinus betulus*) is the traditional medium for creating a stilt hedge, which is a dense clipped screen as thick through as a standard hedge but supported on trunks that are bare to a height of about 1.8m (6ft), so allowing air and light to plants at lower levels, as well as removing the sense of complete enclosure created by a conventional hedge.

A pleached screen is one in which branches are trained so that they extend only to the left and right of the main stems along the line of a row. It is usually created with a form of lime (*Tilia platyphyllos*) using a row of matched plants, evenly spaced about 3.5–4.5m (12–15ft) apart. A classic pleached *allée*, with a row on each flank of a path, has historical links suggesting grandeur and timelessness. It is traditionally composed of limes with trunks bare to a height of about 1.8m (6ft), but a pleached screen can be effective if its branches extend from just above ground level.

Boundary and internal hedges in really rural situations can look more in keeping with their surroundings if they are 'laid' in traditional fashion. The technique of laying a hedge involves cutting and weaving the main stems at an oblique angle, which will cause new shoots to spring vertically from the main stem. It is not difficult to do and can transform an ordinary hedge of upright shrubs into an attractive living screen that is also a more effective barrier to intruders. Cut each main stem three-quarters of the way through, about 23cm (9in) above its base, and bend it to one side about 30° from the horizontal. Hold the cut stems in position with a series of upright stakes, and finish by interweaving long malleable hazel, willow, clematis or briar stems to make a binding at the top of the stakes.

Pergolas are a superb means of defining the space in a garden, making divisions that are more architectural than simple screens, and creating enormous impact while allowing intriguing glimpses of the area beyond. In large areas, they bring human scale to the scene, extending the built environment into the garden and articulating the transition with its mantle of plants. I once saw an imposing pergola, its broad, horizontal timber beams cantilevered from a single line of impressively bold uprights. It was situated so that it closely followed the curve of a lake and its entire length was clothed in immense drooping racemes of lilac wisteria. Its purpose was purely visual, giving scale and perspective to the huge sheet of water. In more moderately sized gardens, pergolas provide opportunities to create many special situations. Sheltering tables and chairs, they can make private, secluded areas or perfect settings for more sociable pursuits because they are open enough to feel airy but dense enough to provide dappled shade from strong sun.

In its traditional freestanding form, a pergola is a covered walkway that frames the views to either side as well as ahead. It is a bonus when the walk is enveloped in climbers, especially the heavier, more rampant kinds such as honeysuckle, jasmine, old rambling roses or fruiting grape vines, their great weight securely supported on the sturdy timbers. A keen gardener will revel in the excuse to put in a range of plants, each one of different, complementary, habit and flowering time, creating a succession of bloom and leaf colour.

It is quite possible to make a pergola in a tiny, restricted space by building it against a wall, bearing the horizontal beams on a metal joist hanger. This overhead construction is a good way to create privacy from neighbours: it impedes their view but still allows light to penetrate the creepers. On upper levels, it can shelter a roof terrace or balcony from sun and wind, creating an intimate hideaway.

An arrangement of timber beams supported on the open side by a rail over vertical columns can be physically strong enough to support a vigorous grape vine or an unbridled flowering subject like wisteria, the horizontal plane being particularly suited to displaying the pendent fruit and flowers. In winter, after leaves have fallen, the bold framework of the plant and the structural form of the pergola will retain a strong visual presence without blocking light from the house.

Timber is probably the most versatile construction medium, easy to cut to shape and freely available in numerous dimensions. The wood should be fully seasoned to avoid twisting, and softwoods need to be treated with preservative, either by a factory process (after cutting, so that there are no untreated ends or surfaces) or locally on site. Though not glamorous in their natural state, softwoods are economical and can be finished in one of the subtle new exterior preservative colour stains, to give them distinction and durability. With thoughtful design and detailing, timber can be crafted into the most elegant forms, a far cry from the rusticated structures so often seen.

Hardwoods like oak are handsome and durable, though costly. They need no finishing and if left untouched will develop the silvery and, to me, beautiful look of wood that has been exposed over the years to the elements. If you prefer a more mellow, honeyed appearance, an annual application of wood oil will do the trick. Although it is not always easy to verify, ask for proof that your timber is grown ecologically and harvested from sustainable sources. It is sometimes possible to obtain recycled timbers that have had a previous life in building or marine construction. I think that there is something evocative about the idea that your pergola may have supported the life of a wheat miller, or seen senior service on the ocean.

In some locations, especially in formal or contemporary schemes, timber can look bucolic or heavy. In these situations, metal, with its combination of physical strength and visual lightness, is required. There is now a wide choice in the weights and finishes of steel and aluminium, although metal constructions are generally more costly and complex than timber ones.

left In keeping with the informality of a wild garden, gnarled, crooked branches of various thicknesses, simply nailed together without joints, provide the supporting columns, joists or main bearers, and cross-beams. This makes a sturdy, rustic pergola that is easily repaired as individual parts age and fail.

below The view to the side of this gracious pergola is as important as that from each end. The substantial overhead structure allows plenty of headroom and easy passage beneath, while the spiralling stone columns form a series of framed pictures as you walk under the mantle of climbers that includes *Clematis* 'Marie Boisselot'.

below Surrounded just with lush climbing shrubs and herbaceous perennials, this single piece of simple box topiary might have little impact. It is restored to prominence through being framed by a timber Gothic arch, even though the arch is painted green and buried like some curious folly.

right Placed in a pivotal position at the intersection of paths, and framing the sculpted centrepiece, a rosy arbour is the focal point of this part of the garden, its importance emphasized by the sentinel pair of evergreen box pyramids. Its slender metal components are light and graceful and allow plenty of headroom, despite the exuberant drapes of ornamental vine.

opposite Against a dark brooding curtain of plantation conifers, a ring of sculpted figures floats on high like some celebratory aerial dance by mysterious woodland beings. Their supports merge with the young trees being trained as pleached standards to produce an eye-catching living gazebo beyond a froth of wild rose bay willow herb.

Hand-forged ironwork is completely at home in more classical designs where it can be formed into intricate patterns to complement the details of a period building.

Where a lighter or more temporary effect is desired, steel wires may be tensioned between walls or within a freestanding framework of posts. For new minimalist gardens, stainless steel rods and wires enable the creation of cool and clean structures of surprising strength. The effect appears almost invisible, leaving plants seemingly suspended in space. Featherweight, pale grey aluminium can be spun into fine tubular forms or cast into framework. By contrast, the meant-to-be-rusty appearance of oxidized steel, beloved of sculptors and architects alike, can look brutally magnificent combined with stone or concrete in a bold, uncompromising setting.

In addition to the fundamental concerns of enclosure and division, sight lines and eye-catchers are other important elements of good garden design. Without something for the eye to stop and focus on, even momentarily, a garden can seem restless and unsettling. And any vista, long or short, will be more inviting if it leads – either physically or visually – to a destination. Vertical structures – sculptural or architectural – are often ideal, permanent solutions that may be made more interesting or colourful with climbing plants through the seasons. Structures can also be used to frame a focal point or decorative object, and thus lend it more importance.

Sometimes a single statement is all that is required. This may be permanent, such as a superbly trained and pruned evergreen arch crowning a statue, or a wrought-iron arbour swathed in honeysuckle, or a trio of simple trellis pyramids, supporting different varieties of clematis, used as part of a border design.

Portable plant supports make splendidly flexible eye-catchers. They can be moved around according to season or mood. Used in conjunction with containers, they can change the look of a courtyard or terrace several times each year. When hosting annual climbers, they will fill a mid-season gap in a border of perennials where spring bulbs have died down.

focal points and eye-catchers

Obelisks, cones and columns run the gamut of styles from formal structures of timber and metal to casual hazel teepees. To be architecturally correct, the obelisk has a square section that narrows toward the top, terminating in a decorative finial. In general they look most at home in formal or classical settings, but when made of unfinished, rough timber they also suit more casual situations. Cones and spirals play similar visual roles. Made of stylized metalwork, they can be used formally in symmetrical pairs, or more informally in unmatched groupings to support lightweight climbers. In a contemporary garden, spiralling wands of reflective steel will introduce brilliant touches of light, while rusting industrial elements like springs and reinforcing rods can be incorporated into funky, sculptural forms.

Beautifully woven willow wigwams, which have a relaxed feeling that gives them a place in any style of garden, are now widely available. For an easy or rustic scheme, especially for annual flowers that are discarded at the end of the season and so do not need long-lasting structures, try making them yourself. Wigwams can be made from hazel or dogwood stems, bamboo thinnings or any suitable shrub or tree prunings, held together with soft young stems of willow or with Japanese-style knots of dark string. A cone of wooden battens or dowelling, nailed to a small wooden disk at the top, would be longer-lasting, and almost as simple to assemble. Painted a bright colour, it would bring height, contrasting texture and a splash of colour to an informal border or vegetable patch.

In whatever shape or form, permanent plant supports take on important architectural roles and should be built with conviction. Simple designs usually work best. They allow easy access for pruning and training and, especially for deciduous plants, look clean and uncluttered in winter. Make them physically and visually strong, using materials suitable for the purpose. In a permanent position, they need to support heavy stems and withstand buffeting winds, so adequate foundations and firm fixing are crucial. Extra care taken at the design and installation stage will be repaid in spades with durability and appearance.

To merit its place at the back of a border, where height is already emphasized by trellis-capped fencing, upright shrubs and majestic mulleins (*Verbascum bombyciferum*), any additional vertical structure needs character and special visual appeal, or it will disappear passively from view. This slim cone of steel rods, topped with a decorative finial, has the timeless quality of an alchemical device while providing plenty of support for the slightest of climbers.

Style is subjective, influenced by our nature, where we live and our personal experiences. By their habit and form, plants have their own spirit and represent different moods – spiky and sharp, soft and opulent, flamboyant and carefree – and what you choose to support them will complete your own particular gardening style. Whether cool and restrained in the city, or unrepentantly romantic in the countryside, a host of twiners and scramblers can be given a role to play in your garden.

Romantic expression is given full vent in this archway smothered with luxuriant foliage. Hinting at the wisteria that flowered earlier in the year, and the vines that will colour later, it is now suffused with deliciously scented honeysuckle.

formal

Symmetrical layouts, with clipped topiary, avenues and coordinated beds providing an atmosphere of ordered calm, are the hallmarks of classic formality. But a formal design can also be excitingly effective when the geometry is redefined by curving arches and stylish pergolas supporting a flow of exuberant planting.

above A cascading raceme of white wisteria is the epitome of elegance in a formal climbing design.
right A restrained colour scheme reinforces the poised calm of this intimate courtyard where the space is defined by a framing pergola and an enclosing screen of bold grid trellis, backed by huge clipped topiary evergreens.

Formality in a garden depends on an underlying sense of order, and one dependable way to introduce this is by establishing a symmetrical arrangement of regular shapes and structures. You can use a whole repertoire of traditional vertical components to create calm and balance in gardens that reflect historical periods and trends. However, a formal garden can also be an expression of bold contemporary thinking and can include more innovative, even daring design elements.

There is a host of vertical statements that can establish or, more gently, suggest formality in a garden. Structures include trelliswork, arches and arbours, pergolas and rope festoons, and purpose-made frames in geometric or representational shapes. If well designed, they will have their own sculptural value in the garden, whether or not they support climbers. Living architecture in the form of evergreen topiary, sculpted hedges and trained trees is also redolent of formality.

Trelliswork, or treillage, is perhaps the most commonly used means of achieving a formal atmosphere. It is not only relatively inexpensive and erected quickly, but also a remarkably versatile medium. It lends itself to any number of design options from enclosing a whole small garden with screens to forming a component of arches and obelisks. Trelliswork has a long history, with humble origins as a strictly functional support intended principally for grape vines. By the seventeenth century, it was being used in grander gardens as a favourite device in the construction of highly sophisticated garden architecture. Trelliswork today is recognized as a way of making decorative garden architecture where historical authenticity is the main priority, making it suitable also for post-modern schemes.

Simple trellis panelling fixed on to walls, or used as a means to enclose or divide spaces, bestows an immediate sense of orderly rhythm and requires little skill to install. More expertise is

left Trelliswork is ideal for creating an impressive but light architectural effect. The wooden laths of this open, glass-roofed loggia suggest the columns and niches of a classical façade. Cunningly arranged panels on the flat back wall successfully create the illusion of three-dimensional niches, penetrated by the foliage of climbers.

right Matching panels of closely meshed, painted trelliswork form pierced screens on both sides of a highly ornate period summerhouse. This is an eye-catching focal point, despite its subdued colour scheme, suggesting grandeur and dignity in its raised commanding position. To one side, a clipped sweet bay (*Laurus nobilis*) in a Versailles tub echoes the formal tone.

required, however, to construct an ambitious design to blend with an elaborate feature, such as a pillar, or to fit an alcove. Here, construction is more complex and expensive, and it would be worth the investment to commission a specialist company to provide superior timber and finishing, as well as appropriate detailing, to create a long-lasting and weatherproof design.

Part of trelliswork's unique appeal lies in the tension between its light airiness and the substantial architecture that it can suggest. You can take this apparent disparity further by using false perspective, angling and spacing the individual wooden strips to create the illusion, for example, of a receding vista, a false doorway or a *trompe l'oeil* window or frame for a recessed mirror. This kind of effect is easiest to achieve when carried out on a grand scale, although a scaled-down version can have startling impact in a more modest garden, especially if used as a focal point, or to break up a large wall. Plants can play a

supporting role in creating these illusions, although the effect is often most dramatic when planting is fairly restrained. If you use annual rather than perennial climbers, slender twiners instead of rampant scramblers, you will allow the structure itself to work as an architectural device. Heavy plant cover has another disadvantage: it complicates repainting or repairing the trelliswork.

A dramatic way to underline the formal design of a garden is to embellish or emphasize its main axes, together with entrances, intersections and transitions, using overhead structures that support plants. Quite apart from their architectural value, a great advantage of these structures is that, at a stroke, they transform the garden into a three-dimensional space.

Arches are usually unambiguous, eye-catching accents in the formal garden, and strongly directional, framing a vista or focal point, but they can also act as a screen or division from the side. Choose the site carefully so that the arch seems a natural, almost

formal

inevitable feature. It could signal a transition from one area of a garden to another, for example, or a change of level, or enhance an existing feature like a piece of sculpture or an impressive shrub that might otherwise merge invisibly into its surroundings.

A pergola is a more ambitious structure that compounds the effect of an arch with the repetition of paired supports. In the classical pergola, the columns are spaced out evenly on both sides of a path, and are topped by linking bearers or joists, which in turn support horizontal cross-beams spanning the path. The columns are important, both structurally as supports, and visually because they usually remain more visible than the overhead cross-members, which tend to vanish under their mantle of greenery. Uprights can be made of brick, stone, metal or timber, the last two materials often bedded on a brick or concrete base. Conventional pergolas have horizontal wooden cross-beams and a sturdy appearance, whereas metal structures usually have curved tops and create a more lightweight tunnel.

The word pergola is Italian in origin, and the structure's prime function is to relieve the discomfort of direct sun in hot climates by providing cool shade, often sweetly scented by the climbers trained overhead. It will produce this welcome effect wherever sited: against the house as an open-sided loggia (an ideal site where space is limited), over a gathering place for dining *al fresco* in a larger garden, or across a path, which it will transform into a secluded walk, sheltered by its protective canopy of foliage. The ideal lateral distance between columns is the same as the width of the pergola, but stronger joists will allow this to be increased, a benefit in shady gardens where maximum light and air can be critical for plants.

A more specialized kind of support is festooned rope. The original effect was created in the eighteenth century using a heavy chain suspended between two uprights. Today, tall pillars linked by ropes slung in even, graceful curves are far more often seen. Climbers are trained up the pillars, with their strongest canes and stems then tied in along the ropes, which define the elegant fall of flowery and leafy swags. This kind of divider makes strong, yet somewhat romatic formal lines without obscuring the full view of the garden beyond.

The formal garden is often at its most seductive when there is a balanced contrast between loose or billowing plants and their ordered, symmetrical support framework. Here a series of linked arches, made of enamelled ironwork, rises from brick plinths set to each side of a main axis in the garden. Roses and clematis, always good companions for summer display and continuity, are trained into them.

Even when plant supports are freestanding and used as sculptural elements in their own right, they should be positioned thoughtfully, to enhance a theme rather than overwhelm the planting.

left Gilded columns topped with tilted blue cubes make unusual uprights for a contemporary festoon. The uniform drop of the swags, which are being used to support clematis, helps to reinforce the softly formal character of the garden.

clockwise from top left This is another version of the festoon being used to divide a garden while providing support for plants – in this case a rose trained into the openwork base of a substantial column.

An ironwork column, grille and startlingly decorative finial are rugged elements of this composition, their open structure making it easy to train plants such as clematis through and around them. The blue enamelling of the ironwork and the gilding of the finial ensure that this functional support also plays a full decorative role in the formal plan of the garden.

A cone of metal has its own sculptural value in a smart city garden, but is also ideal for supporting a range of climbers, including, as here, passionflowers.

Ivies such as the variegated *Hedera helix* 'Oro di Bogliasco' weave through this zigzag ironwork railing that is painted a striking colour and decorated with simple but elegant finials.

a timber obelisk

Some gardens or areas of garden, though carefully planned, can lack impact, scale or perspective. Often this is due to the absence of vertical statements. Versatile obelisks can provide the answer. One makes a focal point, four would make distinctive corners to finish a parterre, and two will frame a doorway or entrance, increasing its impact and importance.

This project shows you how to make a stylish timber obelisk yourself at a fraction of the cost of a ready-made one. Though not a project for the complete novice, anyone possessing a good set of woodworking tools and some previous experience can take it on as an exciting challenge. It can be made from softwood that has been treated with preservative or, especially if you want to leave it unpainted, durable Western red cedar. Timber is usualy sold in lengths of 2.10m (7ft) and increments of 30cm (1ft), in a variety of widths and thicknesses; it should be ordered 'planed all round'.

This obelisk can be made simply with four panels of vertical and horizontal slats, securing the faces with pins along the edges and galvanized wire at the top and bottom, finishing with a coat of preservative wood stain. Or you can give it a sophisticated finish with frames that cover and strengthen the corners, and a ready-made capping and turned finial. The final touch is to paint it with two shades of a favourite colour – here we chose lavender.

The obelisk can be used with a co-ordinating square Versailles planter; or positioned on a paved or gravelled surface, in which case a small paving slab or area of gravel must first be removed so that the climbers can be planted directly in the ground beneath. It can eben be placed directly on turf or soil if the corner feet are set on tiles to keep the timber away from direct contact with damp ground, though this is not recommended.

MATERIALS AND TOOLS
2m x 80cm (7ft x 30in) board for template

45m (135ft) of 20 x 10mm
($^7/_8$ x $^3/_8$in) battening for the vertical and horizontal slats

Four 2.10m (7ft) lengths, plus one 2.4m (8ft) length of 60 x 10mm ($2^1/_2$ x $^3/_8$in), and four 2.10m (7ft) lengths of 50 x 10mm ($1^7/_8$ x $^3/_8$in) for the side frames

Four 0.70mm (28in) lengths of 60 x 10mm ($2^1/_2$ x $^3/_8$in) for the bottom rails

Ready-made capping 130 x 130 x 25mm (5 x 5 x 1in) with ball finial

Panel pins 30mm (1in)
Brass or stainless steel screws 40mm (1$^1/_2$in)
Polyurethane waterproof adhesive
Exterior paint in two colours and brush
Tape measure and pencil
Panel saw
Straight edge
Hammer
Pincers
Drill

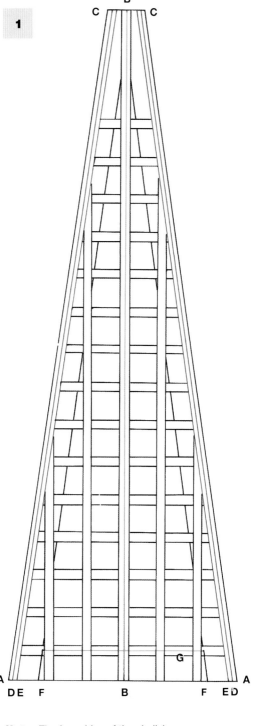

Note: The four sides of the obelisk are made up of four panels. Two of these panels are wider than the other two. This allows the obelisk to form a perfect square section when the narrow panels are fixed inside the wide ones. The overall dimensions are 1.80m (6ft) high, and 600mm (2ft) wide.

1 Mark up a template on a board, following the design shown in the drawing opposite. Start with a horizontal base line, **A–A,** which is the finished width (600mm/2ft). Then make a vertical center line, **B–B,** to the finished height (without finial), (1670mm/66in). Mark the horizontal top line, **C–C,** (110mm/4$^{1}/_{4}$in) and connect the four outer points. Mark the outer edges of the wide panel, **D** (marked in red on the drawing), 10mm/$^{3}/_{8}$in inside the outer lines. Mark the outer edges of the narrow panel, **E** (marked in blue on the drawing), 20mm/$^{3}/_{4}$in inside the outer lines. **A–C** shows the height and outer measurement of the wide side frames (**A–F** is the width of the wide side frame). **D–C** shows the height and outer measurement of the narrow side frames. **G** (marked in green on the drawing) is the top of the bottom frames.

Using a length of batten as a width guide, mark the horizontal and vertical slats, making square shapes of approximately 8 x 8cm (3$^{1}/_{4}$ x 3$^{1}/_{4}$in). Start the horizontals 50mm/2in from the bottom: it does not matter if the top gaps are different in size.

2 To make the first of the two wide panels, follow the lines **D–C** (marked in red on the drawing). Take lengths of the 20 x 10mm ($^{7}/_{8}$ x $^{3}/_{8}$in) batten, and, using the template, mark up the 5 vertical and 15 horizontal slats in pencil and cut them to size.

3 Tack the horizontals into position on the template, but do not knock the pins right in.

4 Dab adhesive at each junction, lay the verticals in position over the horizontals and fix securely with pins.

5 Remove temporary pins from the horizontals with nail pullers and lift the panel off the template.

Make one more identical panel. Then repeat the procedure, making the two narrow panels, following the lines **E–C** (marked in blue on the drawing).

a timber obelisk

6 To make the side frames, cut four pieces each of the 60 x 10mm (2¹/₂ x ³/₈in) and the 50 x 10mm(2¹/₈ x ³/₈in) timber to the length shown **A–C**, on the template. Fix one wide and one narrow piece together at right angles, so that each face is now 60 x 60mm (2¹/₂ x 2¹/₂in), using adhesive and pins.

Repeat so that you have four side frames.

7 Trim the bases and tops of the side frames so that they will sit squarely on the ground and make a horizontal platform at the top. Lay the corner edge of a frame along the outside line of the template. Mark the base line of the obelisk on the outer face.

8 Then mark the base line on the inner face.

9 Turn the frame over and repeat this operation on the opposite side of the template. Connect the marks with a pencil using a straight edge. The angle will then be clearly seen.

10 Cut through the line carefully with a panel saw.

Mark and cut the tops of each side frame in the same way.

11 Trim a small segment off the tops of the inner edges of the side frames to allow the tops to meet. Do this by placing the angle of the frame along the template, marking the vertical centre line, and cutting the small segment off.

Cut four bottom frames (see step 14) from the 60 x 10mm (2¹/₂ x ³/₈in) timber, using the template **F–G**, as a guide.

Paint the slatted panels in the pale shade, and all the other pieces in the deep shade.

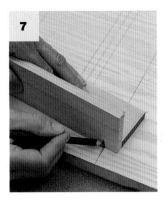
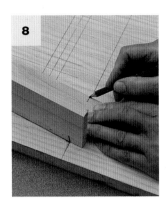
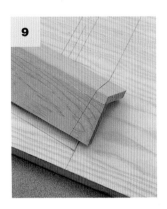

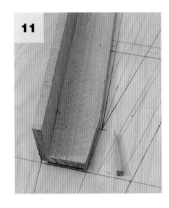

12 Assemble the obelisk with the horizontal slats to the outside. Place the two wide panels opposite each other with the narrow panels facing each other inside them. Fix together using adhesive and pins.

13 Making sure that the obelisk remains square and the sections meet in a neat square at the top, apply the four corner frames. Fix with pins.

14 Fix the four bottom rails with pins.

15 When the the adhesive has dried and the obelisk is firm, apply the capping/finial to the top. Drill through the capping diagonally into the top of the panels and fix with 40mm (1½in) screws. Check, fill and touch up with paint as necessary.

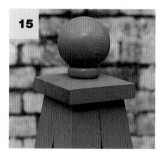

below The formal character of this garden is established by strong, repeated structural horizontals and verticals, against which the informal growth of plants makes attractive contrasts. Narrow columns of Italian cypress (*Cupressus sempervirens*) have been severely trained along the overhead timbers of the pergola to frame the views to the garden beyond.

right An impressive and powerful arch, unadorned except for a dense covering of hornbeam (*Carpinus betulus*), marks the transition and change of level at a small flight of steps. Numerous vertical elements, including obelisks, trelliswork and evergreens clipped as columns, all help to reinforce the atmosphere of calm formality.

There is a huge choice of suitable plants for growing and training on arches. Among the best for formal gardens are those trees and shrubs that lend themselves happily to severe pruning and training, including beech (*Fagus sylvatica*), hornbeam (*Carpinus betulus*) and flowering quince (*Chaenomeles spciosa*). Apples and pears are among the most pleasing and easily trained fruit trees, especially pears which have slightly more flexible stems for manipulating on curved frames. A sequence of fruit-clad arches makes a cool, shady and highly ornamental tunnel, decked out with an exuberant froth of blossom in spring and laden with colourful fruit through summer and autumn.

A well-built pergola can provide support for vigorous climbers. Favourites include wisteria, jasmine, *Clematis montana* cultivars, rambler roses, such as *Rosa* 'Alberic Barbier', honeysuckle and deciduous vines, such as the crimson glory vine (*Vitis coignetiae*). A classic combination for rope festoons is hops (*Humulus lupulus*) and rambler roses. Most strong climbers, especially in formal situations where neatness is important, need cutting back at least once annually to avoid excessive weight and a developing mass of shaded dead growth. This is usually done in winter or early spring, although wisterias and grape vines benefit from more frequent pruning to stimulate flowering and fruiting.

In a formal setting, an excellent alternative to erecting a support with trained plants is to create a living arch of strong hedging plants such as evergreen yew (*Taxus baccata*) or deciduous beech or hornbeam. You could simply cut the opening as an integral part of an existing hedge, but it will look more impressive if the arch is carried above the hedge line and clipped as an upstanding, monumental feature. It is usually necessary to have a framework of stakes and crosspieces to support growth, especially at the outset. You can put up a similar structure over a path or gateway to train deliberately planted specimens as a separate, freestanding green archway.

Hedges are among the most important and widely used living architectural features for adding height and structure, as well as providing shelter, privacy and definition when areas of the garden need to be partitioned. Conventional hedges can be evergreen or deciduous and even flowering, although blossom and fruit sometimes have to be sacrificed by annual clipping in order to maintain a trim silhouette. They are best cut with sloping sides, so they are broader at the base and narrower at the top, allowing all parts of the hedge to get a reasonable amount of sunlight. You can trim the top uniformly to a level finish, but there are many variations that are more exciting, such as crenellations and

swooping scallops. You can also shape decorative finials, which stand above the main line of the hedge to add height as well as ornament. It is easiest to train and trim these into symmetrical geometric shapes such as balls and cones, but if you are ambitious and have a good eye, you could go for birds or animals, for example – or even mythical or fanciful subjects, drawing on the repertoire of freestanding topiary. Create these extensions by allowing selected strong shoots to grow above the line of the hedge, tying them in their initial stages either to canes

Mopheads of hornbeam balance, apparently precariously, at the top of a tripod of stems. This effect is best achieved using matched specimens that have been trained vertically until the stems are well thickened. With their lower shoots removed to leave bare stems, the trees are replanted to form the tripod, neatly reinforced and ornamented with evenly spaced ties.

or poles inserted vertically through the hedge, or by dispersing shoots and tying them around pre-formed frames made from wire or bird netting. You can remove these supports once the finials have been established, or leave them buried in the foliage.

Permanent supports are often necessary for more elaborate creations, such as the hornbeam grid (seen above right), or where you might decide to use plants such as honeysuckle that are not self-supporting. Ivy is a very popular climber that is increasingly used for training as fast-growing topiary and to make a 'fedge' – that is, a fence with the appearance of a live hedge. Root cuttings from the mature flowering form of ivy produce strong woody-stemmed plants that will develop into a low, self-supporting hedge. Juvenile forms need training on a fence of wire netting or chain-link mesh: tie or interweave the pliant stems until the wire is hidden beneath a dense mantle of foliage, then it will

need trimming only twice annually, once in late spring and again in late summer.

The simplest and most popular topiary shapes are the low spherical ball and the standard mophead, which is a ball formed at the top of a single, straight stem with its sideshoots removed. Box, hornbeam, beech and holly make excellent subjects. Standards are most effective used in containers for framing entrances, though low balls growing directly from the ground work well in a defining role set alongside a path.

Topiary – the art of clipping evergreen trees and shrubs into shapes – is a historic way of using plants as sculpture and has long associations with formal gardens. The first records of this esoteric but satisfying practice date from Roman times, although the technique was elaborated into its most sophisticated form in the gardens of Renaissance Italy. With their arresting stone

structures adorned by sculpture, these gardens remain the inspiration and primary reference for classical grandeur and formality, which was further emphasized by the use of topiary for green architecture and eye-catching features.

Plants for topiary must respond well to regular clipping, forming a dense uniform surface. Those that grow rapidly are at a disadvantage because they need frequent trimming, often several times in a single growing season, if the shape is not to be quickly lost. For this reason, privet (*Ligustrum ovalifolium*), for

A sturdy framework of stakes and crosspieces rising above this hedge of hornbeam supports main stems trained vertically, with horizontal arms extending to each side. To maintain the regular, clean lines of this grid the supports need to be kept in place – but they soon blend with the developing hornbeam growth – and all the sideshoots must be kept well trimmed.

formal

example, is not an ideal subject, even though it is versatile and will support larger simple shapes. For large-scale pieces yew (*Taxus baccata*) is often the best bet, while box (*Buxus sempervirens*) is traditional for smaller and highly detailed designs. Both can be trimmed to a variety of geometric shapes, including obelisks, cones, spirals and balls, while more ambitious possibilities include simple representational shapes such as birds, animals or even fantastical pieces like railway engines, much favoured in the 1950s.

You can train topiary specimens without an upright or framework, using the plant's own woody habit for support. In the early stages, however, it is helpful to use canes to position projecting elements such as a bird's tail, while netting, wire and ironwork frames have the advantage of showing the finished shape before the topiary has matured, which has practical and decorative merits. Even when the topiary is complete, the frame forms a core that guides very precise trimming and supports the sometimes precariously balanced mass of stems and foliage.

You can achieve formal geometric shapes similar to those produced by topiary techniques using climbers trained over large frames such as the obelisk described on pages 34–7. A wide range of pre-formed wirework frames is available for popular shapes, or they can be custom-made from metal. The plants that are most widely used for this are small-leaved common ivies (*Hedera helix*), which grow fast to produce a dense face of evergreen foliage. Climbers such as clematis and passionflowers (*Passiflora*) are also suitable. They are much looser in form but have the advantage of producing showy flowers, which is an ornamental bonus for simple abstract forms.

Alternatives to topiary or climbers trained on frames are shrubs and trees of naturally regular form, requiring little or no pruning to retain their characteristic shape. The range of taller plants with distinctive outlines includes those that are typically layered or tiered (such as *Viburnum plicatum* 'Mariesii'), weeping (weeping birch *Betula pendula* 'Tristis') and columnar (golden-leaved *Taxus baccata* 'Standishii'). All are immensely effective for adding individuality to the garden's vertical dimension.

The appeal of this garden lies in the contrast between the woodland backdrop and the solemn assembly of dark, formal topiary shapes in yew, and the lower domes of clipped box that dominate the relatively small, pale contemporary terrace. The tall sculptural forms at the perimeter are defined from the outset by metal frames, which will give precisioned containment to the yew as it matures.

styles

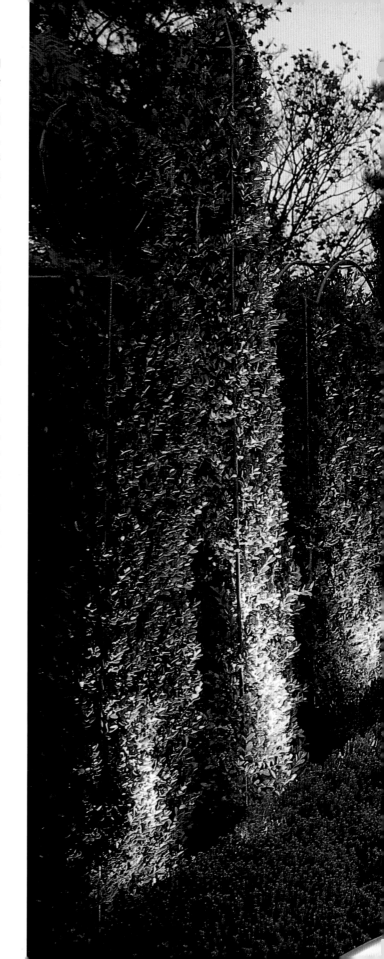

romantic

Romance is a stone archway adorned
by the velvety beauty of an old-fashioned
rose, a large-flowered clematis emerging
through the filigree of an ornamental
trellis, or an arbour so overgrown with
ivy and honeysuckle that it becomes a
secret refuge. Integral to the effect are
voluptuous layers of softly muted colours,
sweet scents and a sense of natural,
seemingly unconstrained planting.

left A slender metal pergola supporting *Clematis montana* rises gracefully from a sea of pastel-
coloured planting at Giverny, in France, which includes sweet rocket, alliums and mauve hesperis.
above Double-flowered *Clematis* 'Comtesse de Bouchard' comes into bloom when the montana is over.

Climbing plants are the very essence of romance in the garden – tumbling over walls, massing in soft billowing clouds, cascading from trees, partially obscuring the view to give the onlooker the thrilling sense that there are hidden mysteries and secret groves beyond. Almost as important are the structures that support these plants. Mellow brick and old stone walls, elegant trelliswork screens, pergolas and arbours, gazebos and pavilions are the very underpinning of romance. No garden lacking vertical interest or upright elements can be romantic.

Romance can begin with the exterior of the house itself. Expanses of wall give the perfect excuse for vegetative decoration. This is especially welcome on newly built houses, which can look brutally exposed in their early years. Why wait for natural weathering to soften the effect when climbers can do the job within a couple of seasons? Deciduous Boston ivy (*Parthenocissus tricuspidata*) is particularly good in this role: the new spring foliage emerges soft pink, turns bright green in summer, and then to fiery reds and ambers in the autumn. The mature, deeply dissected foliage is slightly leathery, causing a rattling sound when assaulted by wind, while young trailing shoots shiver their tiny foliage like curtains in the breeze.

For sunny walls, try the trumpet vine (*Campsis radicans*), which to me always suggests the luxury and indulgence of the French Riviera during the 1920s and 30s. Triumphant shoots of warmest, pinky-orange blooms leap out in great profusion from a mass of many-toothed leaves from late summer to autumn, bringing a glorious finale to the season. Shady walls can be covered with brightly variegated ivy, such as *Hedera helix* 'Adam' and 'Eve' or the romantically named 'Oro di Bogliasco'.

There is a tendency to panic about the potentially detrimental effect of clinging climbers on walls, but as long as masonry and finishes are in sound condition in the first place, problems are restricted mainly to clearing any invasive shoots from gutters and window frames. But if you are worried about damage to your

walls, install supporting wires or trellis panels, held away from the walls by battens, and grow twiners on them. White or pink *Clematis montana* will gallop away in pale swathes in spring, the white-flowering potato vine (*Solanum jasminoides* 'Album') produces frothy masses of star-like flowers from late summer until the first frosts, and, in between, the early and mid-summer clematis species show off blooms in every shade of white, pink, purple and blue.

Roses are, of course, the true romantic's flower. To look great on house walls, they must be grown en masse, so choose clustering forms, scented where possible, to make a really dramatic sensuous statement. Some of my favourites include 'New Dawn', which freely produces heavily scented, palest pink blooms, deeper pink 'Zéphirine Drouhin', 'Bobbie James', which needs space for its generous trusses of semi-double creamy-white flowers, and 'Guinée', a ravishing dark maroon, wonderful against a pale wall.

Outbuildings, garden walls and fences provide great opportunities for theatrical licence. Pretty buildings like summerhouses can be transformed into romantic stage sets by sprays of voluptuous old roses. Unattractive or somewhat utilitarian buildings, such as a tool shed, can be disguised with climbers like ivy or evergreen honeysuckle. Naturally romantic structures, such as pavilions and gazebos, can be enhanced with less vigorous flowering climbers like large-flowered clematis.

Entrances are mysteriously inviting when partly obscured by flowers and vines, and I have to confess to the complete inability to cut back either the delicate trailing fronds of Boston ivy that drape my front porch like oriental screens, or the 5m/16ft) tendrils of jasmine that descend from roof level across my windows. For me, they speak of the slightly edgy balance between civilized contemporary living and the primeval forces of nature. To enhance the feeling of adventure, when visitors are expected I light candles in glass lanterns among the foliage.

left A simple timber pergola supporting climbing roses carries the profusion of planting in this informal garden right to the house. Thus the charming tin-roofed cottage becomes integral to the romantic picture.

above, left to right Unashamedly lavish cerise and pale pink roses climb and tumble among unstoppable wisteria foliage to obscure the entrance, smother the garden wall and reach up to the first floor balcony of this pretty blue-and-pink painted house front.
An old-fashioned white picket gate opens to a latticework entrance arch, festooned with sweetly scented jasmine clambering through white roses in front of a white-painted wooden house.
At Giverny, tightly clipped rectangles of Boston ivy reinforce the vertical form of the shuttered window and entrance door, while a simple metalwork arbour supports a canopy of roses.

romanitc

right The gazebo presents an excellent opportunity to make a grand architectural statement. This elegant timber octagon, with a backdrop of tall evergreen trees, serves both as a visual focal point and a link to the romantic garden in front of it. The choice of unpainted hardwood stands out visually, while reinforcing the natural woodland beyond, and the light infill of trellis panels provides support for climbers. The climbing pink rose dreamily complements the surrounding swathed plantings of white marguerites and mauve French lavender.

below A deep veranda, cleverly set over a shallow pool, doubles the size and scope of this tiny summerhouse. It is surprising how many ways found objects can be given a new lease of life. Here, gnarled branching trees have been used as pillars, an imaginative inspiration for the overall design. The romantic effect is heightened by the scented 'Sanders' White Rambler' rose, creeping softly over the roof tiles. The rustic ambience is completed by the intricate seat, fashioned from twisted vines.

right There are times when a simple linear structure works most effectively. This excellent example of a plant support echoes the feeling of a gazebo without its dominant presence. Natural timber sits well in the larger rural landscape, while the boldness and strength of the design, needed to withstand the weight of climbers against strong winds, is refined by the good finial detailing and inset lozenges in the sides. The combined pinks of the simple rose and clematis are all that is needed to stand out against the background of grey-green conifers.

below If nature wants to take over, why try to stop it? The owner of this charming wooden outbuilding obviously agrees with this philosophy: not only are clouds of pale roses, including 'Bobbie James', encouraged to climb all over the walls and roof, but a trellis screen to the side is gradually allowing the plants to envelop the whole garden. The pale colours of paintwork and climber set off the rich plant combination below, including more roses and lavender.

romanitc

left A rustic arch has been given a subtle twist by a sequence of ladder-style uprights that support single overhead beams, creating a pergola festooned with cascading roses that include 'Reine des Neiges', 'New Dawn' and 'Pink Cloud'. At the end of the vista, a round window of woven stems allows a tantalizing glimpse of the countryside beyond.

below Arches are excellent for framing a view or creating a transition from one area of garden to another. On this framework of timber battens, decorated and strengthened by a cross bracing of latticework slats, twining wisteria meets up with a decorative vine, to provide spring and autumn interest.

Softness, lushness and a sense of nature left to run free are intrinsic to the style of a romantic garden. This does not mean that the underlying layout cannot be formal or symmetrical; but, if it is, it must be camouflaged and softened by plants that are relatively unconstrained and allowed to explore their own particular characteristics of form and habit; climbers, in particular, should be free to show their natural inclinations without undue tidying and pruning. In general it is perhaps easier to make an informal garden romantic, and this is particularly advantageous in that it allows the creation of structures, if not exactly at random, certainly in gradual succession.

One arch is all you need when planting your first rose, and though your initial ideas may be quite modest, you can easily extend this structure into a series to become a pergola when your delight in the exploration of new species takes hold. The obvious solutions are often the best, and they don't come much easier than the bones of a rustic arch. Simply take three stout poles, bed two uprights firmly into concrete in the ground

left Almost nothing makes as glamorous a stage effect as a rose arbour. To support such vigorous performers, the structure needs to be really sturdy, though conversely, the more delicate it looks, the more effective its presence will be. Here, the wrought iron, with its strength and decorative lightness, comes into its own, crowned by Rosa 'Félicité Perpétue'.

opposite, clockwise from top left Personal imagination has a big role to play in garden style. To emphasize a creative clash of a magenta rose and purple clematis, a simple metal tripod is topped with a reflective blown glass ball.

The generous white clusters of *Rosa* 'Bobbie James' fulfil a handsome summer role over this strong brick archway, while the creamy margins of evergreen *Euonymus fortunei*, trained here as a wall plant, support the theme all year round. Focus is brought to the foreground by a slim wirework obelisk, its elegant finial emerging from a froth of lusciously pink sweet peas.

When a single focal point is needed to create interest in a border, the wigwam provides a sympathetic solution. This elegant example, made from hazel uprights interwoven with a twisted spiral of willow withies, supports *Clematis florida* 'Seiboldii'.

The stems of old tree ferns – a luxury for most of us – make unlikely supports, but in this garden they have been recycled to become splendidly organic rose pillars. The use of old iron chain in place of tying twine is equally bold and inventive.

and nail the third horizontally across them at the top. But why stop there? Make a second arch or a third – or more, and link them by placing parallel poles from arch to arch into a lovely walkway connecting different parts of the garden, or sheltering or screening a terrace.

If your taste is for something more elaborate, you can easily obtain decorative metalwork arches from garden centres and catalogues – or you may be lucky enough to find a blacksmith who can make one to your own design or one that suits the architecture of your house. A stylized trellis construction will also make an admirable romantic archway or pergola. Choose sawn timber for the framework and apply ready-made latticework slats to achieve a soft but sophisticated effect. You could paint it in a quiet contemporary pastel shade such as lavender or pewter grey and grow clematis in dreamy mauve, such as 'Perle d'Azur', with purple 'Jackmanii'. Another of my favourite combinations for an earlier-season show is the sulphur-yellow centred, deep purple 'Warsaw Nike' with the less vigorous but sensationally flowered mauve 'Mrs Cholmondeley'.

Rich perfume is also a vital ingredient in the romantic garden, so consider planting common jasmine (*Jasminum officinale*) or star jasmine (*Trachelospermum jasminoides*) for their powerfully scented summer flowers. Combine two honeysuckles, *Lonicera periclymenum* 'Belgica' and 'Serotina', to take advantage of early and late blooms, or plant deep pots with old-fashioned heady-scented sweet peas, which can be cut to bring into the house.

Sometimes garden structures can be romantic in their own right, without the need for a covering of climbers. Rococo pavilions and airy gazebos in the classical style and pillars draped with swags of looping ropes or chains are among the most romantic of garden structures. A temporary, tented arbour made from an overhead fabric canopy, perhaps with softly gathered drapes tied to the supporting uprights, will make a picturesque focal point and give summer shade.

In a wide-open landscape, the form and placing of upright structures needs to be treated particularly sensitively. The intention in this wildly magnificent setting was to work very much with nature rather than to impose upon it, while at the same time making a dramatic vertical statement. Single rustic poles, echoing the upright form of the reeds at the pond margin, are linked by loose, elegantly looped cordons of boating rope, paralleling the horizontal line of the shoreline beyond. One end of the rope is graphically twined into a spiral, clinging to the pole like a totem. The other ends in a heavy fringed tassel, which is allowed to swing freely in the wind.

below The flexible qualities of willow (*Salix viminalis*) provide the opportunity to weave a simple or a complex shape, making as light or dense a division as you require. This decorative living screen, planted directly into the ground, combines a low section of criss-crossed stems held in place by a horizontal 'rail' of dried stems interwoven through them, while alternate vertical stems, allowed to grow taller, are twisted together into a series of open crossing arches.

right One of the joys of creating a living arbour or screen is its foliage: the delicate feathery leaves rustle in the breeze while the overall mass of greenery allows dappled sunlight to shine through. This large and dramatic arbour of weeping pear (*Pyrus salicifolia* 'Pendula') takes good advantage of these qualities, making a striking statement in the naturalistic woodland garden, while creating an atmospherically shady shelter for a bench that is especially welcome in high summer.

Natural, organic shapes are romantic in feeling and you can echo them in the design of vertical structures, with wirework and wrought iron being especially suitable where strength and permanence is needed. You can also use natural, organic materials, such as willow, vines and fresh bamboo, to make ephemeral vertical structures. By interweaving the flexible stems, perhaps combining different species to give contrasting colour and texture, you can create imaginative wigwams and screens that are no less beautiful for being transient.

There are situations, especially in an informal or woodland setting, in which built structures are simply inappropriate because of their sheer rigidity. The fluidity and movement of living material fits into the landscape much more sympathetically. The practice of creating shapes from plant material is hardly new, and clipped topiary evergreens like boxwood and yew are very familiar. Recently there has been a welcome resurgence of interest in woodland crafts, one of which is the pollarding of willow trees, especially the osier (*Salix viminalis*), to acquire straight whippy stems, known as withies. When dried, these can be used in basket- and hurdle-making. Feshly cut, they can also be planted straight into the ground and trained into living garden structures. It is also possible to do this with other young and fairly flexible-stemmed shrubs or trees, such as hazels or the various dogwoods (*Cornus* spp.) with colourful stems.

styles

There is also a growing number of woodland craftsmen taking up this specialist art and it is possible to commission them to work with you to develop a unique naturalistic design. Many grow their own willow, enabling them to offer rare varieties with stem colours of purple, black and sulphur yellow. Though these are usually reserved for basket-making, small quantities can add interesting texture and contrast to a construction.

The flexibility of the material allows it to be woven into quite intricate forms, so the structure may be practical or whimsical, or perhaps both. Fencing and screening are obvious subjects, most effective when there is space on either side to show off the summer growth of foliage. These can be graphic criss-cross designs or more flowing, to incorporate woven hearts, spirals, butterfly wings or any curving shape that appeals to you. The beauty of using a deciduous tree is the fact that the pure design shows up in winter after leaf fall, while in summer the luxuriant foliage comes into its own.

You could try making something yourself, perhaps starting with a small screen at the back of a border or a simple obelisk. However, if you are feeling more ambitious, you could make a arbour to shelter a seat. As you will see on the following pages, the procedure is very simple. The stems are just pushed straight into damp ground where they will root readily, but remember that they can only be established in late winter when the willow is cut.

romanitc

a living arbour

This project shows you how to make a woven willow arbour, which will be an enduring delight. When covered with summer foliage, its leaves rustle gently in the breeze, while sunlight creates lovely moving shadows. After the leaves drop in winter, the tracery of the interwoven stems makes a delicate architectural statement. It is designed to shelter a comfortable bench, and will make a striking focal point. It will be a fixed feature, so select a site with care, preferably one from which there is a pleasant view.

Though at first the project may look daunting, the principles and method are simple, needing only patience and a good eye. It can help to have another pair of hands to hold the stems together while you are tying them.

This particular arbour measures 2.5m (8ft) from side to side, about 90cm (3ft) from front to back, and about 2m (7ft) high, although it can easily be adapted to a smaller or larger size. The ground plan is a semi-oval, but it could be a full semi-circle. It is made from freshly cut stems of willow (*Salix viminalis*). The flexible qualities of this willow have made it the preferred choice, when dried, for weaving baskets and making woven fencing screens over generations. It is fast-growing and takes happily to being pollarded; its growth regenerates each year after cutting, making it an economically and ecologically sound material.

Willow stems are very easy-going and root easily when freshly cut, especially in moist loamy soil. To help a poor soil, incorporate a couple of barrowloads of organic farmyard manure two weeks before planting. It is best to avoid very sandy, fast-draining soil, or very exposed situations. The project must be carried out in late winter/early spring using 'green' willow before it starts sprouting. When they are newly cut, these year-old stems, or 'withies', should be very supple, so it is not normally necessary to soak them in water before planting. However, it is important to cut at least 2.5cm (1in) from the base of the stems, back to fresh wood, just before planting, to ensure that they will make roots.

Water the arbour directly after planting, and then continue to water regularly for the first six months whenever the weather is dry. In late winter, prune the sideshoots back tightly to the main stems in order to expose the beauty of the framework. Growth will commence in the spring, starting at the top.

After two years the arbour will have become well established with shade-giving, leafy growth covering the framework. It will continue to mature, building up a really strong and majestic structure.

MATERIALS AND TOOLS

2 willow stems, each 4.5m (15ft) in height x 2.5cm (1in) diameter at base

9 willow stems, each 3.5m (12ft) in height x 2cm ($^3/_4$in) diameter at base

20 willow stems, each 3.5m (12ft) in height x 1cm ($^1/_2$in) diameter at base

25 willow tip cuttings, each 75cm (30in) long

12 marker sticks

Secateurs
Steel spike 2cm ($^3/_4$in) in diameter 1.2m (4ft) long, with pointed tip
Strong natural twine for tying
Coloured twine for marking out
Tape measure

1 Mark out the ground plan. Using marker sticks, measure out the 2.5m (8ft) width of the arbour in a straight line, with one stick at each end and one in the centre. Mark the depth (front to back), about 90cm (3ft), directly behind the middle stick.

2 Mark out a shallow arc, using a futher 8 equally spaced sticks. Use a measure and string to make sure that both sides of the centre curve evenly. With the metal spike, make vertical holes 30cm (12in) deep at all the markers.

3 Make the vertical framework. Push one 4.5m (15ft) willow stem into each of the holes at either end of the arc. Gather the tips together, crossing them over where they meet at the top. Tie together with twine leaving the long tips loose.

4 Insert the 9 thicker **3.6m (12ft)** stems at their markers. Starting with the middle stem, bring each one forward and tie in to the others.

5 All the stems should be tied together at the apex.

6 Twist and knot any loose tips to an opposite stem. Continue until all the tips are secured. The vertical framework is now complete.

7 Start to weave in the diagonal framework with the thinner stems. Insert two of these, equally spaced, between the first two verticals. Cross them over each other and then over the verticals at 60cm (2ft) above ground level, one over and one under the vertical.

8 Take the end of the stem that is now crossing the outer vertical and wind it round the outer vertical to reinforce it.

9 Take the other thin stem and nterweave it, diagonally towards the back, over and under the vertical frames it crosses. Repeat with two more thin stems on the opposite side of the arc. (It is easiest to weave using the full length of stem rather than working with just the tip.) Then insert two thin stems between each of the remaining verticals, weaving them diagonally across the framework. The weaving becomes finer towards the top as the stems narrow.

10 Secure the diagonals to the verticals at all the crossing points. Take a thin willow tip cutting 75cm (30in) long and form a short U at the cut end. Holding this against the junction, wind the long end around several times, leaving the base of the U exposed.

11 Finally push the tip through the tie to make a secure knot.

12 Finish the completed tie neatly to give a good decorative appearance.

13 Repeat this operation until the whole structure is interwoven. Now firm the ground around each stem by stamping down.

14 Secure the apex by interweaving loose ends at the top into the outer two vertical frames.

15 Tie the central top point securely with twine, and then trim off any ends that cannot be woven.

16 With a long tip cutting, interweave a decorative ball to cover up the string ties. Begin and finish by inserting the ends into the twine ball.

urban

Urban spaces offer particular vertical
challenges – and rich rewards – to
the gardener. Even in the tiniest of city
back yards, imaginative use of the
vertical plane can generate interest
on many levels and help to create an
enclosed refuge from the frenetic
pace of city life.

left Ladders, raised walkways and beds in many layers expand this small town garden into a
fascinating multi-dimensional recreational space for children and adults to explore. The spare,
angular geometry is lightly softened by wisteria and other climbers, sensitively trained to avoid
diminishing the effect of the clean architectural lines.
above Despite their exotic appearance, passionflowers are tenacious and tolerant of city air.

left Bold ideas on a large scale can be highly effective in a confined space. Here a wide, wisteria-clad arch frames Corinthian columns dramatically supporting the contorted limbs of an ancient fig tree.

below Carefully chosen elements contrive to make a calm, Japanese theme in a small urban garden. A slatted fence with a delicate covering of climbers shelters rocks and low-growing, mound-forming plants, dominated by perennial grasses.

We live in a busy, industrialized world, bombarded constantly with fast-moving images, noise and distraction. The need for a place to escape has never been more pressing; but, especially for city and suburban dwellers, gardens can be very restricted by their surroundings. Apartments are carved out of large dwellings previously occupied by a single family; new houses are squashed into a space that was once a garden; and areas formerly the province of warehouses and factories are now developed into a multitude of homes. High walls emphasize the potential claustrophobia of narrow, shady spaces. The solution is to exploit the vertical dimension to its maximum, training climbers on walls and screens, arbours and obelisks. Plants will play a pro-active role in the creation of this refuge, introducing life force and a more congenial microclimate. The structures that support them can also play a part, as aesthetic features in themselves.

Space is at a premium in the city, and urban gardens are typically small and enclosed. Every inch of space matters, and vertical structures and climbing plants can make a bigger impact than they would in larger, more open situations. However, making the most

urban

of every inch doesn't mean busily filling every inch, nor does a small space mean that everything in the garden must be small-scale. A balanced, harmonious theme or a heroic, dramatic gesture can work wonderfully in an urban context. Lines can be pure, materials positive: for example, wires tensioned between steel girders forming screens for privacy, or bold, reclaimed timbers supported on concrete posts to make audacious arbours.

Urban gardens, perhaps more than any others, tend to be extensions of the houses to which they are attached, and the design and style of the structures and planting will reflect how they are used. Some town gardens are designed chiefly to make a beautiful picture when viewed from the house, although they may be used for entertaining when the weather is fine. Their setting is carefully staged, and a formal, orderly style is often the most effective, with neat, regular fencing or walls, and elaborate treillage or topiary. The arrangement of plants and structures can be symmetrical, with geometric or repeated patterns of planting and pliant woody-stemmed climbers, such as euonymus, laburnum or espaliered apples, fairly rigorously trained, often on ornamental supports such as obelisks. If the garden is to be used more regularly, like an outdoor 'living' room, the layout can be more informal or, if it is formal, softened by lush, flowing planting. There should be room for seating and a table for relaxing, eating and working outside, and the overall atmosphere of the garden shoulld be relaxed, too. Plants such as sweet peas, hops and the cup and saucer vine (*Cobaea scandens*) can be allowed to grow in a more natural style, freely scrambling over a variety of supports. This arrangement will also suit a garden for plant-lovers and those who want a space that will bring a little of the artless charm of nature into the more rigid architecture of the city.

Screening is vital in urban areas to shield the garden from the outside world – primarily either for privacy from close neighbours and surrounding buildings, or for protection from winds on high-level terraces. Seating areas particularly benefit from shelter and enclosure. Boundaries can be clothed with a profusion of climbers such as fragrant honeysuckles, jasmine and small-flowered clematis to engender the sense of intimacy and seclusion in an overlooked garden, while the garden itself can be carefully arranged to focus attention inward, with focal points, specimen planting, beautiful arrangements of pots and containers or man-made structures, perhaps painted in jewelled colours, to arrest the eye.

A solid screen can cause problems, creating a feeling of entrapment by blocking out light and air or, in exposed locations,

left On this city roof terrace a climber-covered arbour shades and shelters a seating area, providing a haven of living greenery among the surrounding built environment, while more open views are allowed in the rest of the garden.

below A sheltering arcade protects a handsome wooden seat from being overlooked in a formally laid-out city garden. The beautifully balanced design, the handsome pergola and the matched paint effects all ensure attention will be held within the garden.

urban

67

stopping winds dead and making them swirl into unpleasant currents that eddy round corners, causing icy draughts just where protection is most needed. A barrier that filters wind and light will be much more effective.

Very interesting woven and knitted steel meshes can be made into sophisticated and unusual screening. For a technical look, stretch the mesh over a framework of bright metal; for a gentler effect, use natural planed hardwood. Front this with tall zinc troughs planted up with Virginia creeper or espalier-trained cotoneaster or flowering quince to reflect the structural geometry. Flat metals perforated with geometric shapes make a stylish alternative, though because of their smooth surface it is not so easy to get climbers established on them; however, you could suspend containers at high level, allowing parthenocissus, small-leaved ivies and other foliage creepers to cascade into a cool living curtain, flowing in the breeze.

For a sophisticated, low-budget screen, make the framework from seasoned softwood painted black or dark grey. Cover the frame with fine chicken wire, folding and tacking down the edges to avoid sharp points, or use grey nylon fly screen net. The plant supports can be made from nylon fishing line, pulled tight in close, horizontal rows.

Screens that alternate between open plant supports and solid panels can be very useful where a certain amount of shelter is needed but you don't want totally to block a pleasant view – for example, from a roof terrace. Alternating panels of pale fabric and

left and right These are two very different but equally effective solutions for very similar confined spaces. Both are enclosed, use raised planters and have a decking floor. In the garden on the left, however, all the boundaries are camouflaged. The sides are covered by exuberant natural planting of mainly upright plants such as bamboo, phormium, sansevieria and grasses; and the back is completely disguised by a mirrored metal backdrop which gives the impression that the garden extends beyond it. In the terrace on the right, on the other hand, the elegant enclosing trellis is meant to be seen. It is decorated, rather than hidden, by climbers and trained shrubs such as camellias and ceanothus and, along with the striped, perfectly matched planting boxes and the pattern of the decking, contributes to the formal effect.

wire are effective but ephemeral; you can create the same impact by building a longer-lasting solid structure, without losing the sense of lightness. A bold timber framework of vertical posts can be linked visually by a continuous top and bottom rail. The plant training sections could be made from horizontal slats or dowelling, and the wind screens from panels of glass or PVC. Depending upon the desired look, you can make the frame from inexpensive softwood stained with a colour – a subdued greyish-mauve looks cool. For sophisticated urban chic, natural planed hardwood finished in a protective oil looks especially smart framing round-section brushed-aluminium bars for the plants.

A sheltering pergola, perhaps constructed from lightweight aluminium poles, creates excitingly graphic shadows on walls and floors. Electric down-lights will extend the dynamic effect through the evening, especially when casting the decorative leaf silhouettes of climbers like Boston ivy, passionflower or the enormous heart-shapes of crimson glory vine (*Vitis coignetiae*).

As a material for man-made structures, metal is a favourite in contemporary minimalist garden design, a style that can be highly convincing in an urban situation. Tubes and angle-sections can be engineered into boldly dynamic shapes – frames, boxes, pergolas and obelisks – to suit strong-growing formal climbers such as clematis or evergreen, white-flowered trachelospermum. Tall rods of twisted, shining steel make interesting vertical landscape among smaller-growing twiners. Metalwork armatures and topiary-style shapes can form arresting statements when

a spiral sculpture

There is something quite magical and almost primeval about spirals. They appear in so many life forms: they exist in the internal structure of mollusc shells; underground water courses flow into them; even the casts thrown by earthworms form into them. Spirals seem to transmit energy, and plant tendrils naturally coil round like springs, firmly clasping their hosts. It was this force and form that inspired me to use the type of 'hourglass' bedsprings that are normally used in upholstery. They are available from good craft shops or upholstery suppliers.

It is a free-form structure, which seems to have a will of its own, making it amusing though sometimes frustrating to work with. For this reason we give an outline and the principles of this project's construction so that you can proceed until you like the result.

We have given the structure a contemporary organic look, using a tall but slender pale-coloured terracotta pot to show off the free-form nature of the coils and also because it is not too heavy to be brought indoors during cold winters. It is planted with the lovely scented twiner *Jasminum polyanthemum,* chosen because it is delicate enough to follow the curves. More springs can be added as the plant grows, though it can be kept in check by regular clipping, which also helps to promote profuse flowering.

The project can easily be adapted to 'grow' directly out of the ground and will look most effective if formed into an oversized clump. The informality of annual climbing nasturtiums, *Tropaeolum majus,* would work well in this situation or, in order not to overwhelm the overall construction, yellow canary creeper, *T. peregrinum* or flame red *T. speciosum.*

MATERIALS AND TOOLS
At least 20 steel wire 'hourglass' bedsprings
Fine galvanized wire for tying
Heavy galvanized wire for fixing
Wire cutters
Fine pliers

1 Begin by connecting two springs to form a right angle from their bases. Cut a piece of wire 15cm (6in) long and with the help of pliers, start winding in a neat coil around the base of one spring. Now hold another spring tightly at right angles to it and wind the wire around that in the same manner. Cut off the excess wire and squeeze in the tip with pliers to neaten.

2 Connect more springs in this manner to form a platform for the structure, consisting of 4 verticals with 2 horizontals.

3 Continue building up the structure with verticals tied together with horizontals. Because of the inherent springiness, the structure will feel quite 'lively'. Make the ties as neat as possible, to suggest the twining tendrils of an exotic climbing plant.

4 Continue building upwards and sideways until you feel satisfied with the overall form. Fix the structure into a pre-planted container with 30cm (12in) long pieces of heavy-gauge wire bent into a narrow U shape 2cm (³/₄in) wide, pushing them in on the diagonal for extra security. Encourage the plant into the form so that it can make its way upwards as it grows.

planted with climbers. The larger-flowered clematis cultivars – 'Mrs Cholmondeley' or 'Warsaw Nike', for example – look most impressive when grown over conical spiral forms or large spheres and boxes.

To create suitably cool structures, the light-reflecting, smooth appearance of stainless steel and aluminium, either polished or spun, comes into its own. The desired effect may be ephemeral, with mesh-like sculptural confections floating like clouds or tensile wings, articulated by stretching tendons of wire. A web of taut wires spun around a steel framework can be formed into pyramids, cones or flying sails as backdrops. Plant with a drifting ampelopsis, white passionflower or, in warm climates, evergreen *Ficus pumila* to suggest gentle movement and grace.

Where you want a bolder though still visually light look, creating hollow pillars of square wire mesh can increase the apparent weight of the construction. Planted with climbers, a freestanding row of these, arranged like organic sentry boxes, will

define a pathway, or – placed adjacent to the wall of a tall building – emphasize the building's height, or frame doorways or line windows. Tendril climbers like passionflower and the cup and saucer vine work well, as they will fill the space easily, can be restricted to the shape of the form and still show off their sophisticated flowers all over the surface.

If metal seems too hard or too cold, a softer and warmer but still contemporary-looking material for fences, screens and plant supports is bamboo. The strength and rigidity of bamboo has made it a favourite construction material throughout southeast Asia, where it grows abundantly. In Japan, it has reached a high art form, and is used traditionally for fencing and gates in temple gardens from Kyoto to Tokyo. It is found in a wide variety of designs, from cross diagonal latticework to complex arrangements of verticals with thatched borders. One of the most notable features is the distinctive way in which the bamboo poles are tied together, using thick black string tied into elegant knots,

spaced evenly and each one identical. Though some persistence is required, it is usually possible to obtain bamboo in a number of heights and thicknesses from specialist suppliers. Finding the right string is more of a challenge: I find that dark-coloured tarred twine is a good option, or natural sisal for a paler finish.

Bamboo is particularly suitable in an urban setting, giving a subtle oriental touch while maintaining a clean, contemporary appearance. It works especially well combined with decking, stones and water, resulting in a cool and calming ambience. To make a screen to support climbers, a rather open effect is desirable. Using your imagination to create a pleasing design, working out construction possibilities on paper, is a lovely challenge. I am fond of a technique known as the 'four-eyed fence'. Poles of equal thickness, say 3cm/1¼in, are used. Start by tying the horizontal poles to good-looking timber posts, set firmly in the ground, or bolted to a low wall. The horizontals can be spaced apart equally, but for a high screen the best effect is achieved by grouping them in twos or threes. The design is completed by the verticals bamboo poles. These should be tied to the horizontals in groups of twos or threes; each group should be slightly apart from each other, and on alternate side of the horizontals. Tie with individual knots at each crossing point. The effect is something like a piece of single-colour tartan.

All kinds of structures based on this method are possible, perhaps combining different thicknesses of bamboo. Thick poles can be split in half vertically to form a surface finish over a flat panel, or used whole and cut with slots to retain rails.

This garden presents an uncompromisingly modernist picture, echoing the clean, restrained lines of the architecture. The rectangular shapes of the tubular metal frames support carefully trained weeping silver pear (*Pyrus salicifolia* 'Pendula'). They are underpinned by the contrasting curving forms of the low-growing box hedging. The inspired use of climbers and supports – essentially rectangular design elements – complement and reinforce the horizontal building lines.

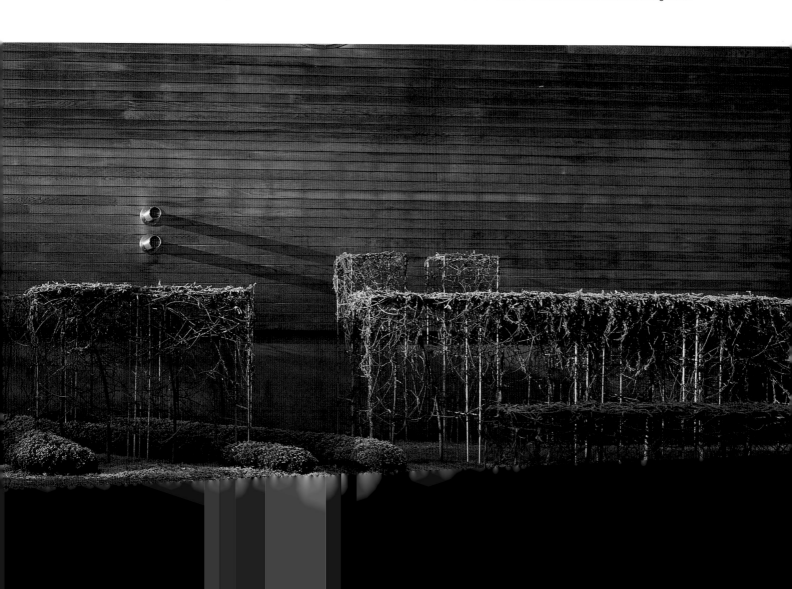

Traditional materials, such as trellis, make effective plant supports. However, the advance of technology in the manufacture of metals, plastics and glass allows for exciting new possibilities when creating structures. The combination of visual lightness and physical strength is a major feature of steel and aluminium, while man-made plastics can be formed into delicately textured textiles and complex coloured mouldings.

left In a plantsman's garden, beautifully designed and ornately cut woodwork is painted in soft green and blue, blending perfectly with the masses of plants it carries.

opposite, clockwise from top left Jokes and surprises can play a significant role in garden style: here blue and silver recycled CDs are strung into a startling, light-reflecting screen that also serves as a support for runner beans in the summer.

Light canvas drapes replace climbing plants to bring mystery and shade to a contemporary arbour that terminates in an unexpected wall formed from dried maize.

A screen of widely spaced painted wooden posts is tied together with barely visible steel wires to define a boundary without interrupting the view beyond.

Billowing wire mesh shapes, like a pile of giant air cushions, form an intriguing tunnel walkway for invading creeping plants.

a contemporary screen

Industrial materials are perfect for achieving a sharp, technical look, and they are extremely effective in contemporary and urban settings. Steel and metalwork constructions tend to be commissioned from specialist workshops, making them less accessible to ordinary garden owners than equivalent timber items. However, we have designed a project that you can easily make yourself, using materials available from your local metalwork supplier, hardware or pet shop. It is a plant-climbing screen that can be used in conjunction with a long, tall planter or set directly into a planting bed. Several of these could be set side by side to provide low-level shelter on a terrace or block out a view.

The screen is made from a framework of non-rusting aluminium rod (available in 4 or 5m-(12 or 15ft) lengths), which can be bent without the use of heat or unusual force. The infill mesh is a type usually used for the construction of aviaries and rabbit cages, and is malleable and easy to bend. You can easily adapt the dimensions to different lengths of aluminium rod and widths of mesh.

We have used the distinctive and appropriately wiry plant *Muehlenbeckia complexa*, but you could plant a light tendril climber like *Solanum jasminoides*.

MATERIALS AND TOOLS
Solid, round-section, aluminium rod, 8mm (³⁄₈in) in diameter, and 7.3m (24ft) long

A roll of 19-gauge galvanized wire netting, 90cm (3ft) wide, with rectangular mesh 12mm (¹⁄₂in) x 2.5cm (1in)

Coil of 12-gauge galvanized line wire

Wire cutters
Measuring tape
Protective gloves

1 Mark the rod into three sections that will form the top and sides of the frame. The width of the frame should be equal to the internal width of the planting container, and each side equal to the depth of the planter plus the height of the screen, so that the two sides also form prongs that are pushed into the planter to anchor the screen. This screen is 85cm (33in) wide and 1.5m (5ft) high, with 57cm (22in) prongs. Bend the rod into shape using a convenient former such as a balcony rail or the edge of a firm table or workbench.

2 Unroll the mesh on to a flat surface to measure the amount required to fill the screen, with an extra 5cm (2in) overlap at the top for folding and finishing, and about the same amount at the bottom for pushing into the soil. (If your frame is wider than the width of the mesh, you can lash two widths of mesh together using the galvanized line wire.) Cut across close to a horizontal strand so that no jagged ends of wire are left exposed.

3 Lay the frame over the mesh and, in order to keep it square on the mesh, tie the frame temporarily into position at the corners with pieces of light wire. Starting at the sides, fold over the overlap mesh round the aluminium rod frame, squeezing it down firmly, and then fold the top, finishing the curves at the corners neatly. The mesh is malleable and easy to bend.

4 Cut the wire into manageable lengths of about 60cm (24in) and lash the mesh to the frame, taking the wire through each hole at the sides and every two holes at the top. As you work, leave 10cm (4in) wire free at each end. When the mesh is bound all round, twist these loose ends firmly together on the rear side, trim them back to 2.5cm (1in) and fold down neatly.

5 Push the frame into the rear of the ready-planted container and tie the plants into position on the screen using 5cm (2in) pieces of cut wire, finished by twisting together at the rear of the mesh.

living

Some of the the most intense pleasures
of the garden lie in being out there, living in
it, either sharing it with friends and family –
enjoying a leisurely lunch, or an intimate
dinner by candlelight, beneath a vine-
covered pergola – or revelling in the joys
of quiet solitude, reading while enclosed
in the perfumed shade of an arbour
veiled in scented plants.

left Handsome painted timber pergolas, festooned with vines and creepers, enclose a section of a
garden to create a secluded courtyard of water, shaded paths and seating areas. The bold
rectilinear lines of the structure frame the living area and the garden beyond.
above The climbing rose 'Phyllis Bide' proclaims summer with suggestions of unfolding richness.

For most of us, simply being in the garden is a pleasure. Each new day is a delight when experiencing birdsong with the first rays of the sun, becoming aware of newly opening blooms in the midday heat, or basking in the heady scent of jasmine and nicotiana wafted on the evening breeze. Just being in the open air is much more enjoyable than being cooped up indoors, and so it is ideal to treat the garden or part of it as an 'outdoor room' – a place for relaxing, playing or entertaining.

It is important to make a link between the home and the garden if you are going to incorporate part of the garden into everyday life. Access needs to be easy; for example, doors from a living area or kitchen leading on to a patio, and the outdoor area will usually need some protection from sun or wind and a visual connection with the house. The most convenient and versatile solution can be a planted pergola to provide year-round shade and shelter on a terrace adjoining the house.

Space for seats, tables and chairs is vital, whether you plan to have permanent outdoor furniture or whether it is an area for impromptu moments when unexpected guests arrive or when children playing outside can't bear to go another minute without food. Large-sized plots and rural locations are certainly not prerequisites for an outdoor living room. A tiny patio or roof terrace will easily accommodate a small table and chairs, and a narrow balcony makes a ready-made location for a pergola to provide necessary summer shade and, just as importantly, a sense of enclosure, with its associated feeling of intimacy and protection. Each of these sites lends itself perfectly to containment as an outdoor room, where privacy can be enjoyed, screened from the eyes of onlookers. City dwellers will especially appreciate the benefits that this can bring to everyday life

A keen do-it-yourself enthusiast can easily create a simple timber structure from off-the-shelf components; or, if that seems too overwhelming, a contractor could be commissioned to build a custom-designed one. For those who are less ambitious or are budget conscious, a framework of wires supported with steel poles should not be too daunting a project, though climbing plants are heavy, so the strength and stability of the structure have to be borne in mind.

This sunken terrace links a garden room with the owner's studio nearby. The pergola, imaginatively created from disused hop-picking ladders rescued from a local farm, supports a large canopy of golden hop, *Humulus lupulus* 'Aureus', and grape vines that bring dappled shade and atmospheric intimacy to this quiet, relaxing space.

living

right Is it decadence to install an outdoor Jacuzzi or simply an extremely civilized antidote to modern, stressed-out living? Either way – and with an ice-cold drink in summer or hot chocolate under the stars on a snowy night – it is a fabulous way to unwind from work or sport. More than that, it is an experience that is best shared with family and friends. Here, the bold timber pergola and simple trellis screen engender a sense of enclosure without blocking out the sky, while the mass of tropical-looking foliage preserves privacy.

below An exquisite and intimate eating space has been created in this small garden. The brick perimeter wall makes a sheltered backdrop trained with espaliered apples, while a simple metal structure, supporting pears, and a thornelss blackberry, arches over an elegant set of table and chairs. A pair of flowering standard heliotropes in tubs linked to low hedges on either side, make the sense of enclosure complete.

right A solid but decorative Arts-and-Crafts-style construction of oak makes a fitting enclosure for this seating area. With its lines appropriately echoing the form of the elegant curved-back seats made from the same timber, it creates a countrified yet sophisticated meeting place.

below A rectilinear pergola is defined at its outer corners by strong timber posts. Horizontal steel wires, given support at intervals by vertical metal tubes, provide a training device for a vine and pollarded tree that clothe its surface and upper sides. Narrow mesh arches set between the posts at ground level further enhance the feeling of a separate enclosure within the garden. Yellow climbing roses, cleverly combined with suitably delicate lemon-painted metalwork chairs, achieve a bright and fresh effect against the surrounding green planting.

A pergola will provide the perfect setting for a number of different scenes, from informal daytime meals to be enjoyed by all the family to a theatrical supper for friends lit with candles in lanterns hanging from the beams and scented with exotically fragrant incense to deter night insects. A pergola comes into its own in summer, when the weather is hot and plants are giving their best show. However, even in cool weather it can be a congenial setting for drinking hot chocolate following an afternoon walk, perhaps with a gas patio heater or a Mexican stove to bring up the temperature, before finally going indoors.

It is a good idea to combine several different plants on a pergola in order to enjoy a varied seasonal display. Consider adding some appropriately productive climbers where food may be served. Grapes are the traditional choice of fruit, frequently used on restaurant terraces, but if you combine them with fragrance and flowers from other plants, you can achieve a more intense experience. *Vitis vinifera* 'Purpurea' is a lovely ornamental vine that makes a beautiful display of deep red foliage with purple fruits, while contrasting, white-fruiting, *V. v.* 'Ciotat' (formerly *V. v.* 'Apiifolia'), the parsley-leaf vine, gives a rather ferny impression with its deeply divided, green leaves. Honeysuckles have beautiful flowers and heavenly fragrance; they can be untidy, graceless climbers, but if you plant them with a grape vine, their worst points can be disguised.

You could grow your own breakfast with a thornless blackberry like *Rubus fruticosus* 'Waldo'. Or try luscious kiwi fruit, *Actinidia chinensis*, an extremely vigorous species needing a strong, extensive structure around which to twine its woody stems; both a male and female plants are normally required in order to produce fruit, or you could plant a self-fertile cultivar like

'Jenny'. Climbing roses trained up the supporting pillars have the benefit of bold, beautiful flowers that provide a colourful display. Deep cerise 'Zéphirine Drouhin' or even deeper 'William Lobb' would complement the berry, while apricot 'Gloire de Dijon' or coppery pink 'Albertine' would look mellow against the kiwi fruit's reddish hairs. Alternatively, pale 'Madame Alfred Carrière' or 'Alberic Barbier' would stand out strikingly among the dark foliage.

If you have room in your garden, it is also wonderful to have a sheltered seating area away from the house. This can be sited so as to take advantage of the prevailing sun, so that you can enjoy being there at breakfast time, in the late afternoon, or whenever you like it best. For maximum versatility, a solid roof will keep the rain out, while sides that are partly screened or panelled will protect against cool breezes. There are many suitable structures, from the airy gazebo, which can make a charismatic focal point

to enliven the garden and may be an interesting spectacle from the house, to the more substantial summerhouse, which can be a retreat furnished with comfortable armchairs in which to relax with friends or to use as a studio for writing or painting. An enclosed seating arbour can stand alone or be set against a wall or fence where space is limited. It may not have the versatility of a more substantial structure, but it is still a lovely spot from which to enjoy a view or to hide away quietly in the warmth of the sun.

A curvaceous, wrought-iron pergola is positioned to create a light and airy canopy over an antique metal table and chairs, its openwork design romantically displaying the drooping racemes of palest lilac wisteria. An ancient curved glass lean-to is shaded by a vigorous kiwi fruit, *Actinidia deliciosa* (also known as Chinese gooseberry), ready to take centre stage with exotic fruits and dramatic foliage, while the green perimeter includes hydrangea, ivy and viburnum.

living

Scrambling foliage climbers can offer an informal look to spaces like this, giving them a sense of being absorbed into a garden wilderness. You will need some wires on which to get them started if a solid construction is involved, although many plants have the ability to climb by winding around themselves once established. Ampelopsis, or pepper vine, is a luxuriant twiner with large, heart-shaped leaves, somewhat resembling the coarser-leaved hop, a rampant herbaceous perennial, with which it could well be substituted. Both provide a lushly dense cover.

If your taste is for flowers, rambling roses introduce an nostalgic, romantic feeling to an arbour. If they are perfumed, it is a joy to sit beneath them on a warm, still evening. It is hard to beat old favourites like 'Veilchenblau', with its exquisite, delicately scented, grey-flecked blue-violet blooms. 'Félicité Perpétue' with trusses of small, double, pink-tinged white flowers, and 'Madame Alfred Carrière' with heavily scented, larger, pink-tinged white flowers, are both good for a difficult shady position. Roses have little to offer visually in winter, so grow a framework of the later-flowering evergreen star jasmine (*Trachelospermum jasminoides*) to achieve cover all year round.

Garden buildings can make marvellous fantasy rooms, perhaps themed on a favourite place or concept such as a scene from a film, or a holiday beach hut. This might consist of a rugged stone or sturdy timber building that could be used as a practical storage room for garden furniture, or as a private studio in which to work undisturbed, or as potting shed. Onto this you could add a terrace and pergola. For total decadence, you could create a rich Moroccan souk where colour can be allowed to play the leading role. By painting the structure a deep azure blue, glowing aquamarine or spice yellow, you can introduce a glorious sense of pulsating energy into the garden. Style it lavishly, using silvery lanterns, painted pots, intricate metalwork furniture and even

left above Weathered timber posts, strung with thick rope balustrades, define a boardwalk across a tropical bog garden leading to a comfortable hideaway. This gazebo reflects its tropical surroundings, with a solid roof made of old corrugated iron giving both shade and protection from heavy downpours. The reclaimed trees used to support it emphasize the feeling of a shipwrecked castaway's refuge.

left below A simple, zinc-roofed seating arbour is enveloped in creepers that help to create a sheltered and secluded vantage point from which to view the informal perennial planting. Ivy and a vigorous hop, *Humulus lupulus*, reflecting the overall informality of the garden, covers its surface.

translucent drapes to add a sense of mystery while screening out the heat of the mid-day sun. Complete the effect with a mosaic-topped table, jewel-like and glittering, flanked with painted chairs dressed with silk cushions.

If you enclose the space with brilliantly coloured climbers you will reinforce the feeling of exotic extravagance. In a hot climate, you can enjoy the startling pinks and purples of crisp bougainvillea, or *Mandevilla splendens* with its rich pink flowering bells set off by gleaming green leaves. For a tempering element in all this heat, introduce *Plumbago auriculata* with its clouds of powdery blue, and morning glory (*Ipomoea purpurea*), ready to open up its huge mauve trumpets, fresh each morning,

A comparable impression can be achieved in more temperate zones by selecting hardier plants with a similar flower colour range. Start with the huge range of large-flowered clematis with their striking shades of pink, purple, mauve and blue. For example, make a framework of dramatically purple *Clematis* 'Jackmanii Superba' combined with blatantly large and red 'Kardynal Wyszynski' and 'Madame Edouard André', a more delicately proportioned, crimson, to produce a vivid clash of excitement. The delicate, pale mauve-blue flowers of 'Perle d'Azur' will add a cooling touch to the scheme.

Many annuals, or tender species that are normally grown from seed, can also fulfil the exotic criteria. They have the advantage of getting started and growing quickly, which is useful while other plants are establishing themselves. Try the cup-and-saucer vine, which climbs vigorously, making complex, tubular flowers that change in colour from green to purple. Similarly exuberant, and in similar colours, though with even more curiously shaped flowers, is Dutchman's pipe (*Aristolochia macrophylla*), but be warned that the flowers also have a somewhat unusual odour which is not to everyone's taste.

right above This charmingly informal garden is full of suggestions of secret meeting places. Its romantic ambience is especially emphasized by the metalwork arbour that leads to a rustic studio beyond. Roses grow best with the benefit of light and air, so the deceptively fragile structure is a perfect support for the shell-pink blooms.

right below Fantasy and fun can be the key to a successful garden recreation area and this one is designed to look as though it is reached directly from the beach. A stout timber pergola cantilevers from the face of the stone hut, extending to the right on pillar supports. Loosely draped fishing nets give both shade and a seaside atmosphere to the terrace and its inviting hammock.

Free spirited gardens for living, though intentionally seeking an informal atmosphere, can still benefit from the inclusion of structures to give then some defining form and distinctive style. The knack is to introduce contextual surprises, such as a row of stiffly formal obeslisks in a wide expanse of grass or a deliberately rustic screen to separate areas of closely packed beds of low-growing annuals.

left If you imagine this flower garden without the elegant metal support, you will realize the important role it plays both in scale and focus. The striking, uncompromisingly modern form makes a surprisingly satisfying contrast with the soft swathes of perennnial grasses and poppies, while the colour of the clematis that it hosts creates a link to the planting.

right above The vigorous *Clematis montana* has almost totally swamped the secluded niche that it was planted to create. The original intention is re-defined by the pretty metalwork table, here decorated with a tight group of diminutively planted terracotta pots.

right centre In the summer it can be delightful to dine in the far reaches of the garden, to enjoy a sense of freedom away from any hard landscaping. Here, a low enclosure of rustic hurdles surmounted by a dramatic cloud of climbing *Rosa* 'Paul's Himalayan Musk' provides a charming backdrop to tables and chairs set on a meadow-like expanse of rough grass. The white goat adds a fittingly bucolic – and labour-saving touch while it meanders, obligingly grazing.

right below Freestanding vertical structures and climbers can be used to define and set the scene for an open living area. A pair of gleaming steel spirals trained with evergreen ivy and jasmine stand on either side of a quiet seating corner. The framing effect is completed by the backdrop of the softly curvaceous foliage of Boston ivy (*Parthenocissus tricuspidata*), which is showing its warm autumn shades.

living

below Heated Victorian greenhouses used to be known as stove houses because of the constantly stoked furnaces that boiled water for their underground pipes. This contemporary version also has a stove, which serves to keep the temperature up in winter both for the plants and for the owners. Passionflowers, creeping around the walls and roof beams, demonstrate their excellent foliage qualities, while pink blooms dangle from *Passiflora antioquiensis* as it grasps its way along the ironwork roof ties.

right A 'cool conservatory' provides a light and equable place for working or entertaining during the warmer months. So long as it is not used to cultivate exotic species of plants, it needs only enough heat to keep it frost free in order to protect tender garden pot plants, such as citrus or abutilon, through the winter months. This charming example is heated by warm air that comes through the cast-iron grill in the floor. It is festooned with grape vines along one side, arranged in decorative rows, to get the full benefit of sunlight and to shade visitors. Pale blue plumbago, canary yellow abutilon and white lilies make sympathetic companions on the opposite wall, producing such a inviting scene that one can almost smell the perfume of the lilies.

Another way of integrating your home and your garden is to bring the garden indoors. People who live in cooler regions, with long winters and short days, really appreciate the opportunity to acquire a glazed conservatory. The combination of high light levels and sheltered access to plants gives an unquantifiable boost to the spirit. Anther bonus is the wealth of wonderful plants that can be grown in controlled temperatures, allowing cultivation of exotic species that might otherwise only be enjoyed on holiday. Climbers are particularly important for conservatories, both as decorative elements and to provide much-needed shade.

A frost-free, 'cool' conservatory – one that you heat only to ensure a winter minimum temperature of 5C (40°F) – will usually just be suitable for habitation in summer months, but is wonderful for over-wintering tender garden plants in pots. You can grow climbers like twining, white and scented *Jasminum polyanthum*, white and blue *Plumbago auriculata*, and tender evergreen clematis like the yellow-flowered *C. australis* and white *C. aristata*. These will do better (some flowering almost all year round) in a 'warm' conservatory with a temperature at around 18–21C (65–70°F) by day and a minimum of 10C (50°F) at night. This is comfortable for most people and suitable for the cultivation of a host of wild and wonderful tropical flowering climbers. When trained up walls on wires or trellis screens, they will usually reach out to take advantage of horizontal roof bracings and any other innocent host their tendrils can grasp. The results is a glorious riot of colour and texture as each plant fights for space. Be sure to provide adequate water, ventilation and shading, since in hot, arid conditions plants can suffer and pests gain control.

The tender species of passionflowers, with their brilliantly coloured, strangely formed blooms, are among the most exotic tendril climbers. *Passiflora* 'Incense' has enormous purple-and-white striped flowers 12cm (5in) wide; *P. antioquiensis*, known as red banana for the fruit it sometimes produces, dangles dazzling rosy pink flowers, making a superb display when strung across horizontal wires. Prized, tall-growing *Lapageria rosea* is a similar colour, but has waxy bells hanging from stiffer stems and foliage.

Freestanding obelisks or topiary frames in pots make excellent indoor features if you want a more controlled effect. Slower-growing, more restrained species are easier to wind and train. *Hoya carnosa* and *Stephanotis floribunda*, both evergreen twiners with waxy white, perfumed flowers, suit frames well and, for a larger obelisk, *Clerodendrum thompsoniae* makes a fine spectacle covered with clusters of white bracts from which precocious little red flowers appear.

below An elegant, traditional style conservatory is filled with enough light to grow a variety of plants, and also provides a luxurious sitting area for a small city house. It has been given a modern treatment using simple but oversized furniture and accessories. Powder blue *Plumbago auriculata* and rich pink *Dipladenia splendens,* grown in pale 'greige' terracotta containers, scramble up distinctive, pewter grey, wirework trellis panels. They are offset by dendrobium orchids and tiny-leafed *Muehlenbeckia complexa,* which rise from complementary long tom pots.

opposite, clockwise from top left
Decorative plant supports suitable for indoors.

Twisting bright steel wands provide modern, appropriately wiry, supports for the diminutively scrambling muehlenbeckia.

Wirework trellis in the form of a classical vase can be purely decorative.

Brilliant steel spirals, designed to replicate the form of twining climbers, seen here supporting white plumbago, make an original and striking alternative to the traditional obelisk.

A Moroccan metalwork screen, trained with rust-yellow bougainvillea, is a reinterpretation of traditional exotic latticework.

This combination of timber frame and steel infill trellis introduces a bold, fresh approach to obelisk design.

A 'candle tree' could provide a sinuous framework for twiners while serving as a lighting feature in its own right.

planting a topiary frame

Climbers can be trained on three-dimensional structures to show off the plants to full advantage and to create beautiful living sculptures – foliage takes on the shape of the frame and delicate flowers bloom without distraction.

In the example shown on these pages, the tender *Passiflora citrina*, which produces unusual, delicate, yellow tubular flowers, has been trained into a cone. Combined with a chic, contemporary, zinc container and hand-made wire frame, it has taken on an urban sophistication and is ideal for a garden room. In the heated conservatory, exotically perfumed *Stephanotis floribunda* and *Hoya carnosa* would be perfect alternatives.

The planting container is an integral part of the look, especially in a formal situation, and should be chosen to complement its surroundings. In a classical setting, painted wood Versailles tubs make a good choice for weighty and vigorous species trained as a pyramid. A Roman-style vase shape in metal or terracotta would suit a less substantial plant on a lighter, spherical frame.

Experiment with different combinations of frame shape and container. An oversized, terracotta long tom, for example, will create a spare, clean look in a contemporary setting. A pair of these, planted up with white passionflowers trained over large spherical frames, will suggest luxury while maintaining the minimalist style.

The size of the pot and frame should balance each other visually, and also take into account the eventual scale of the fully grown plant. Many climbers are extremely forceful and will quickly outgrow a small pot or swamp the frame so check on the suitabilty of the plant before you begin.

MATERIALS AND TOOLS
Climbing plant
Container
Conical training frame
Sterilized potting compost
Enough broken crocks or gravel to
make a 5cm (2in) layer of drainage at
the bottom of the container
Soft natural twine
Scissors

1 First put a 5cm (2in) layer of drainage material into the container, then plant the climber. Carefully separate the stems, and distribute them evenly. Insert the frame.

2 Wind the longest stem around the frame, following the direction of the spiral. Tie in neatly with twine to provide support, keeping unsightly ties to a minimum.

3 The aim is to achieve a natural effect, so make use of the plant's own means of climbing if possible. If it uses tendrils, as here, gently wind them round the frame.

4 Taking the remaining stems in turn, wind until the frame is evenly covered. Trim the ties and hide them behind leaves. Continue to tie in new shoots as the plant grows.

potager

What is more satisfying,
on a sparkling morning in summer,
than reaping the fruits of one's
labours in a potager garden? Vines of
tomatoes, heavy with juicy red globes,
ripening gourds, sugar peas twining
up wigwams and towers of succulent
melons all combine to produce a
vibrant and tempting display.

left Armfuls of gourds dance like glowing lanterns on an archway.
above The young tendrils of the cucumber strike out to find a suitable climbing support.

Although *jardin potager* is simply French for 'kitchen garden', the term 'potager' is now used specifically for a formal garden, divided into small beds and planted with vegetables and fruit arranged for decorative effect as well as for productivity. The beds are sometimes raised or they may be edged with dwarf herb or evergreen hedges, embellished perhaps with corner finials of taller plants such as standards of sweet bay (*Laurus nobilis*) or slim obelisks of rosemary (*Rosmarinus officinalis*). The centre of each bed is often defined by a formally trained fruit tree or an ornamental support structure. The remaining space is filled with a rotating, varied pattern of vegetables, herbs and flowers.

The opportunities for using climbers in a potager are infinite. Growing crops vertically makes the best use of a small space, maximizing yields and relieving plants from competition for light and air, while providing vertical impact without compromising the essential feeling of formality. You can sculpt fruits such as apples, pears or red currants in a range of decorative forms that provide freestanding vertical accents on their own stems; cane and bramble fruits offer seasonal interest when trained on permanent, strong metal or timber structures; and climbing or twining vegetables supply a changing landscape as their temporary supports are moved annually from bed to bed.

The successful design of a potager depends on simplicity and cohesion, using upright features as focal points to draw the plan's components together. (The satisfying impression of pattern and balance is lost if the plan is over-complicated.) Each bed

comprises three key elements: a disciplined edging of uniform plants, the main filling or 'ground' of low or medium-sized plants, and a centrepiece to provide height. You can vary this basic composition according to your taste, inspiration and preferred gardening style, as well as the crops you would like to grow.

Some climbers, for example, can be planted in the beds for training over arches of slender rustic poles to span paths and their intersections, adding cottage garden charm to the formal layout. You might divide beds diagonally in half or quarters with short rows of canes to support runner beans and other annual crops, producing a more traditional kitchen garden appearance with shelter for neighbouring plants as a bonus. You could even erect a simple arbour in a corner or to one side, supporting a

canopy of vines, honeysuckle and climbing beans to shade a seat where you might rest and survey your work.

Remember, though, that vegetables and fruits are seasonal. Few are evergreen plants, and although the potager will certainly be a bustling patchwork of beauty and bounty in summer, once harvesting is finished its continuing impact will depend almost entirely on sound design and solid perennial plantings. Trained climbers need to be strategically placed and carefully pruned so they make an aesthetically pleasing impact even when dormant and leafless. Light, temporary supports will be cleared or stored away, leaving permanent timber or ironwork structures that are durable, good-looking and imaginatively sited to punctuate the potager with a winter focus.

left Trimly edged raised beds echo the crisp geometry of the perimeter fencing. The corner fruit beds are protected from birds by architecturally elegant cages, which dramatically contrast with the rustic informality of the hazel wigwams that support seasonal twiners.

above Where ground space permits, clipped hedges can supply softer boundaries for square vegetable beds, here linked by a soaring archway for fruit and climbing squashes. A tepee of coppiced poles makes a proud centrepiece for climbing beans.

potager

Many vegetables are grown 'on the flat', in rows or patches in the main body of potager beds. Several kinds are climbers by nature, however, and their twining or sprawling habit can be exploited to create living sculpture that adds vitality and height to the edible landscape.

Peas and beans are popular and colourful climbers, easily grown in fertile, deeply cultivated ground, and yielding huge pickings of tender juicy pods or sweet, protein-rich seeds. Peas are scramblers, hoisting themselves up netting or twiggy sticks by means of leaf-tip tendrils. Most kinds today are dwarf or semi-dwarf, commercially developed for easy mass-harvest, but older maincrop varieties are still available. An attractive climber is the classic mauve-flowered mangetout 'Carouby de Maussane' growing 1.5m (5ft) or more to produce strong leafy vines with attractive blossom and large green or purple pods.

Climbing beans, on the other hand, are twiners, their vigorous stems exploring and coiling round any nearby branch or pole in their race to reach the sun. Supports must be sturdy and dependable, for the vines billow with foliage that is heavy when wet and vulnerable to high winds. Some gardeners successfully grow beans in the same place every year and construct permanent wigwams and fences of squared timber or metal pipework for them. Beans can also be sown in fresh ground each year, trained on seasonal supports of bamboo canes or coppiced poles. They will even ride 'piggy-back' on other plants, twining happily up sweetcorn stems, for example, or strings suspended from fruit tree branches.

Squashes, gourds and cucumbers are trailers rather than true

climbers, but their long pliant stems and tendrils help them to grow upwards. If they are tied in to arches, tripods and trellis, they can develop into tall, eye-catching features, contributing a tropical blend of lush foliage, gaudy flowers and large, often extravagant fruits to the potager community. They are grown as much for their great decorative potential as for their produce, and deliver lavish dividends in return for a little simple soil preparation and a warm sheltered position.

Although they are not true climbers, most tomato varieties are 'indeterminate', growing to an indefinite height on a single stem that can be tied to a strong cane or stake, or to wires and strings on walls, pillars and tripods. Sideshoots are normally removed, but you can leave a few to develop into auxiliary stems, allowing you to train plants into decorative fans, espaliers and arches that look spectacular when laden with their trusses of red, orange or yellow fruits. There are hundreds of cultivars, many 'heritage' kinds that need conservation, and it is possible to grow a wide selection of varied colours and flavours as summer highlights or seasonal living fences in a potager.

Even though some of these vegetables are truly perennial, they are usually grown as annuals, from seeds or bought plants, and moved round the garden to fresh sites each year to avoid a build-up of problems and depletion of essential nutrients. They are hungry too, requiring very fertile soil to fuel their often prolific growth, so you will need to cultivate the planting site thoroughly, adding plenty of nourishment in the form of garden compost, well-rotted manure or fertilizer. If starting from seed, either sow where they are to grow, a few weeks before the last frosts, or sow under glass in small pots for hardening off and planting out when conditions are warm enough. Young plants are often available from seedsmen and garden centres, ready for planting straight away, if you are unable or disinclined to propagate your own.

Where possible, install bamboo canes, coppiced poles and similar seasonal supports before sowing or planting, to avoid any growth check from root disturbance. Permanent structures, such as joinery tripods or obelisks and timber or tubular arches, should also be erected well in advance and consolidated or concreted in before the soil is prepared and fed for sowing or planting. Uprights can be wrapped in sleeves of netting or mesh, or strung with vertical wires or cords for tendrils and twining shoots to secure a purchase. Horizontal wires about 45cm (18in) apart on walls and fences are ideal for securing climbing stems, or canes to which stems are attached, with wire rings, plastic twists or loops of soft string.

left Stout wigwams of 2.5m (8ft) bamboo canes or coppiced hazel, larch, willow or ash poles are extremely practical climbing supports for runner beans, teamed here and there with a few tall nasturtium plants. The structures are bound tightly together at the top, and reinforced below by woven bands of slender hazel, willow, honeysuckle or thornless bramble in order to keep the poles evenly spaced. The wigwams relieve the flat uniformity of the lower plantings and catch the eye as they stand tall like patient sentinels.

below A similar rustic wigwam is fitted this time with tiers of horizontal cane spacers and planted with a mixture of edible and sweet peas. It is beautifully positioned to supply a strong focal point in front of the screen, giving the path a destination and contrasting effectively with the angular pots of standard grape vines. The waist-high enclosure of hazel basketry panels is an imaginative disguise for a compost heap.

Apples are a superb sculptural medium. The tiers of branches of an espalier (**above**) echo brick courses and revel in a wall's stored and reflected warmth. Although visually complex, an espalier is simply managed as if each 'arm' were a separate cordon. Cordons – straight stems, grown upright or obliquely – can be serially planted to create walls of blossom, transforming a plain path into an inviting avenue (**below**). Pairs of cordons may be trained to meet overhead as an arch (**opposite**) or, if repeated, as a tunnel or colonnade. Pears and quinces also excel in these roles, their spring blossom even more exquisite and their yields enhanced by close pruning.

Trained fruit trees are classic architectural elements of kitchen gardens and potagers, their strong woody framework of trunks and branches adding a reassuring promise of permanence and continuity. Apple espaliers, pear arches and plum fans are long-term tenants of the garden, requiring very thorough soil preparation and robust supports, able to withstand severe weather conditions and large enough to accommodate annual extension growth as plants develop. In return, trained fruit trees crop heavily and offer aesthetic pleasure at every season – from spring blossom, through summer leaf-cover and colourful autumn crops, to the winter symmetry of their bare branches.

Immaculate early training produces these architectural branch patterns. While they are still young and flexible, shoots are tied in regularly to wires or nails, or along bamboo canes secured to wires as guides for the ribs or arms of the proposed shape. Bending and tying are supplemented by pruning in mid- or late summer, intended partly to redirect or check growth, but chiefly to encourage fruitfulness. Cutting the tip off a main apple or pear stem, for example, will stimulate the development of sideshoots, which are in turn shortened to create stubby spurs on which the flowers and fruits form. Use these spur-trained tree fruits for large features and major elements of the potager design – as decorative cover for high walls, for flanking a pathway to make a floral and fruiting avenue, or to clothe arches over paths, intersections and entrances.

Some tree fruits, such as apricots, plums and acid cherries, do not crop on spurs. Their pruning focuses on tying in young shoots to replace fruiting stems cut out each year after crops are gathered. They are not suitable for tight, strictly defined features, but make good candidates for more relaxed romantic fans on old brick walls. Bush fruits like gooseberries and red currants, on the other hand, are spur-pruned in the same way as apples. Their smaller scale suits them for training as short standards, miniature fans and espaliers on low walls or pathside wires, and rows of cordons for internal 'fences'.

Soft fruits such as blackberries and kiwi fruit are vigorous and very effective climbers, provided that their twining or arching stems are trained and tied promptly to wires on walls, fences, arches or pergolas. Like all fruit, they need plenty of sunlight and benefit from having their stems fanned or spaced out to avoid overcrowding. Choose thornless or cut-leaved forms of blackberries, and leave space for their new canes to develop while the previous year's are still fruiting (raspberries behave similarly). Old canes can be cut down in the autumn.

The first priority is practicality when designing supports for climbing fruit and vegetables. Any structure must be strong enough to bear the weight of the wet leaf canopy and a possibly heavy crop of produce – not just passively, but in the face of strong winds too. It must be sited where sufficient light, air and warmth are available to the plants. It should also be solid and durable for long-lived climbers like tree fruit and grape vines, or easily dismantled for crops that need annual rotation to fresh soil.

Twiners on walls need timber battens, trellis, vertical wires or ropes, all held away from the face of the wall to leave a small gap behind for ventilation. Tendril-climbers prefer panels of mesh or netting, which offer a good spread of anchor points, while plants that are not self-supporting require horizontal wires or a wide-meshed latticework of thin treated timber.

Coppiced poles and other lightweight supports may be simply inserted 45cm (18in) into the ground, with the soil packed down firmly around their base. Permanent, more substantial structures for heavy climbers need to be set in concrete. Alternatively, you could fit 8–10cm (3–4in) square timber uprights into metal spiked sockets driven into the ground. Natural poles do not require any preserving treatment, but machined timber should be pre-treated or painted with a non-toxic preservative after completion.

With technical criteria satisfied, you can plan the aesthetic impact of climbing structures. Simple, elegant materials are most effective and provide an airy outline structure, leaving the plants to supply form and mass. In urban areas, where natural wood may be hard to find and look inappropriate, machined or manufactured materials such as steel, aluminium, wrought iron and finished timber often harmonize best with the surroundings.

Country potagers and cottage gardens, on the other hand, benefit from the sense of place offered by rustic work – slim branches that are sometimes peeled, but ideally still bear their bark, which offers a rough, secure purchase for climbers. Coppiced hazel, willow and ash poles, usually readily available locally, may be used for seasonal and long-term constructions, although they have a limited life-span and should be renewedl after a few years. As a bonus, using natural materials for building supports provides creative opportunities to use traditional binding, weaving and latticing techniques.

Natural timber and stone are the preferred materials for plant supports in this rural setting. Woodland thinnings, natural poles arched and joined, provide the bare bones for structures such as a simple arbour, an apple-clad archway and even a pitched roof capping a quartet of leafy stone pillars.

Natural wood, cut at its various stages of growth and maturity, is a pliant, organic medium, used by gardeners, since ancient Egyptian times, to build pergolas, colonnades and other, simpler structures for supporting climbers. A sensitive material, it imports a breath of the country to the garden. Coppiced poles 5cm (2in) or more in diameter are used for the main uprights of a tripod or wigwam (**left and opposite bottom right**); these will be about 3 years old for willow or hazel, 5 years or more for slower-growing ash or chestnut.

They can be joined by a variety of methods. Galvanized pins or strong staples can be used for thicker material – for fastening poles to a timber post, for example, or joining split chestnut slats to make a latticed panel (**opposite top right**). Where nailing is not feasible, thin rope or strong tarred twine is used to bind and knot poles together, especially for weight-bearing joints or where several poles meet (**left**).

Perhaps the most satisfying method is to use thin, freshly cut stems of vines, honeysuckle and Virginia creeper, or long slender wands of weeping willow or hazel. These need to be straight, free from kinks and sideshoots, and still 'green' enough to bend easily with a slight twist. You can then ply and braid them like rope, or lash and knot poles with them, as you would with string (**opposite top left**). They can even be woven or looped into simple rings and wreaths. Thicker wands, about 3m (10ft) long and 2.5cm (1in) thick at the butt and tapering to a thin whippy end, can be woven over and under poles for textured basketwork, brightly tinted if coloured dogwoods and willows are used (**opposite bottom centre**).

a rustic gazebo

You don't need a large space to grow fruit or vegetables successfully, and if you can fit only one major feature into your garden, you could create an unusual architectural structure that is also productive. This rustic-chic gazebo was designed to form the centrepiece in a new potager but could equally well be set in a small courtyard garden, surrounded by rectangular beds of perennials and herbs, or even as an eye-catching focal point in a larger, more informal layout.

Unashamedly inspired by the constructions i n the restored gardens at the Priory of Notre Dame d'Orsan in central France, featured on the preceding pages, its particular charm is the combination of classical form interpreted in wild and rustic materials. It is simple to make, with dimensions orginally defined mainly by eye, and you could create it on a larger scale to frame an entrance gate or an intersection of two paths. This one is made of hazel stems, but any equally strong, easily available, local timber would do.

We chose to plant a fruiting grape vine (*Vitis vinifera*) and a self-fertile kiwi (*Actinidia deliciosa*), positioned on opposite corners, to grow up and over the roof, though just one of these would be enough if you desire a lighter cover. A thornless blackberry (*Rubus fruticosus*) and a tayberry (a result of crossing a raspberry with a blackberry) are planted to grow like pillars on the other two corners. As alternatives to these, you could choose other climbing plants that would be appropriate for a vegetable garden, such as runner beans and a variety of gourds; or you could mix in decorative plants, such as sweet peas or nasturtiums, with the edible plants. You could also reinterpret the idea for an entirely different type of garden, painting it a vibrant colour and clothing it in deep-hued perennials.

As long as the basic framework is strong and functional, you can let your imagination run free with the decorative touches. You might like to add binding vines around the joints and incorporate found objects like a bird's nest or attractive seed-heads and nuts or, on a different theme, top it with a fanciful finial.

MATERIALS
4 rustic timber posts, each 2.5 m (8ft) long, about 10cm (4in) diameter with the bases trimmed to spikes, and flat tops

8 stout, straight hazel stems, about 1.8m (6ft) long and 2.5cm (1in) in diameter

Bundles of straight hazel stems 1.5–1.8m (5–6ft) long and about 2cm (³/₄in) in diameter

An off-cut of timber 5 x 5cm (2 x 2in) thick, 10cm (4in) long

Stout galvanized nails, 4cm-(1³/₄in) and 10cm (4in)

Found materials for decoration; these could include long willow shoots, old ivy stems, long vines, lichen-covered twigs, berry twigs, discarded birds' nests, discarded bird feathers.

TOOLS
Saw
Wooden mallet
Steel-headed mallet
Hammer
Heavy-duty pruners
Pruning knife
Curved willow cutter's knife (optional)
Tape measure
Spirit level
Tough safety gloves

Preparation

Measure up the site to fit the roof frame; ours measures 1.5 x 1.5m (5 x 5ft) square. Dig over the planting area, incorporating plenty of well-rotted, organic farmyard manure if available, or substitute a bulky mushroom compost.

1 Make the roof frame. Saw 4 pieces of the stout hazel stems into 1.5m (5ft) lengths to make the roof frame, making a diagonal cut at each end so that they will lie flat to form mitred joints at each corner.

2 Laying them on a level surface, nail through each corner to join them into a square frame.

3 Trim the remaining 4 pieces of the stout hazel for the sloping uprights into 1.8m lengths (6ft), again cutting each end diagonally. Nail the top of each one loosely to the corresponding face of the square finial post.

4 Nail the other end of each one loosely on to the square base at each corner, allowing them to project over the base by 10cm (4in).

5 Re-check for alignment to the site, check the assembly is squared up and make any adjustments necessary. Nail all the pieces of the frame firmly into permanent position when you are satisfied with the fit.

6 Add the roof horizontals. Apply the thinner hazel stems in parallel sequence on one side, spacing them about 15cm (6in) apart so they cover the frame evenly. Measure the length of each one by eye against the frame, allowing for a small overhang of 1.5cm ($^1/_2$in) at each end, and cut the ends diagonally with heavy pruners. Nail them into place at each end, making sure that they run parallel to the square base. Continue on each side in the same manner, fixing them beneath their right-angled partner on one corner, then above them on the next so that the opposite faces match.

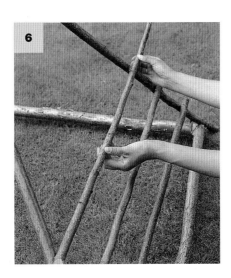

7 Add the decoration. Dress the roof informally by weaving in long vines or old ivy stems.

8 Decorate the finial by winding a willow withy or any suitable vine around it. Secure the loose ends by pushing them under the wound stems.

9 Add any 'found' treasures like this disused bird's nest and attractive chicken feathers.

a rustic gazebo

10 Putting in the corner uprights. Treat the part of the posts that will be below ground by letting them soak in a bitumen-type wood preservative for 24 hours. You can simply dig a hole and drive the posts 45cm (18in) into the ground with a heavy wooden mallet, checking the vertical with a spirit level and then firm back the soil, treading in with your feet.
Or, to extend the life of the posts, you may set these into a bed of coarse aggregate concrete, mounding the concrete just above soil level, and, once you have checked the next step, allowing it several days to set thoroughly.

11 Lay a straight edge over each face and check that the tops are horizontal.

12 With the help of assistants, position the roof over the posts.

13 Securing the roof is best done with the help of two assistants. With one person holding the roof in position, another should hold the first corner steady from the inside and press a steel-topped mallet against the top of the post against which the third person can hammer. This enables the third person to hammer six 10cm (4in) nails into the post, three through each side of the base of the roof. Repeat for the other three corners, checking the alignment as you go.

14 Plant and tie in the climbers. Tie in the longest shoots loosely to the posts with soft twine by wrapping the twine once round the post first, and then a second time round the post and the plant. This method reduces unnecessary damage to the stems as they grow. Water in thoroughly after planting and continue to tie in shoots as they grow.

The sheer scope and diversity of climbing plants allows you to interpret your own individual style on every type of structure you can possibly envisage. Whether draping an arbour with garlands of sweetly scented blossoms, smothering a pergola with brilliantly coloured blooms or clothing a wall with a dense mass of luxuriant green foliage, climbers will provide you with an astonishing choice of subjects. Whatever your location, and whether indoors or out, climbing plants offer a multiplicity of form, kaleidoscopes of colour and layers of texture right through the gardening year.

The fame of the wisteria-clad footbridge at Giverny does not in any way detract from the breathtaking beauty of the pendulous white blooms of *Wisteria sinensis* 'Alba', especially as captured here, with soft mist rising from the water and backlit by hazy morning sun.

P L A N T S

When choosing plants, it is important to take into account the ways and means that they are to climb, and match them to the most appropriate support.

Scramblers and thorn-bearers naturally hoist themselves up through the branches of other shrubs, and when placed by a wall or other structure they need the help of training supports tailored to their less independent habits. Thorny-stemmed roses and bougainvilleas, for example, will make large, bushy mounds on the ground unless their heavy, springy stems are firmly arranged and tied in to tensioned horizontal or vertical wires.

Self-supporting climbers employ a variety of stratagems. Using tendrils to gain height is perhaps the commonest method, with leaves modified into thin wisps that nod in the breeze until their sensory hairs make contact with a possible support; they then quickly curl around it, forming wiry corkscrews that are difficult to unwind without injury. Tendrils will happily grasp single wires, a coarse mesh or trelliswork, or branches of other plants, making it possible to train them on the widest range of supports, including walls, arbours and wigwams. Grapes and other heavy vines, such as the crimson glory vine (*Vitis coignetiae*), and bulky climbers like passionflowers need to grip sturdy supports with their tough springs, whereas delicate sweet peas can catch the finest string with their soft, elastic tendrils.

All the climbing clematis family use leaf stalks like tendrils to grasp the slightest of supports. Wherever the middle of the stalk makes contact with a surface, it wraps itself around several times, clasping the support tightly. In this way clematis can be grown on rods, trellis or mesh, but the stems develop rapidly and should be trained in evenly to prevent dense tangles from forming.

Self-clinging climbers like Virginia creeper have tendrils with tips that swell into tiny cushions. Where these touch a firm, even surface such as a wall, fence or even glass, they produce a strong adhesive and then flatten out to form tenacious suckers. Ivy and climbing hydrangea produce aerial or 'adventitious' roots along their questing stems, and these attach themselves firmly to rougher surfaces. Both types may need tying in to canes or wires for a season or two until they are established.

Finally, the twiners – including such plants as honeysuckle, jasmine and runner beans – produce growing tips that are stimulated by light, so the stems gently bend to follow the sun until they make contact with a branch or pole, which they promptly coil around, leaving the tips free to move on in their upward quest. Most kinds are vigorous, some becoming woody and heavy with age, so substantial supports are necessary.

above Climbing roses form long stems that respond well to pruning, which suits them to this tightly bound spiralling arrangement that has transformed simple poles into an original and sophisticated obelisk.

opposite Deep pink, twining leaf stalks distinguish the tender evergreen *Clematis uncinata* (**top left**), whereas the kiwi fruit (*Actinidia deliciosa*) (**centre top**), climbs by twining stems. Twiners need supports of a scale suited to their vigour so permanent woody subjects need robust structures, while the annual runner bean (**top right**) and morning glory (**bottom left**) can make do with a string or slender pole. *Hedera helix* 'Ora di Bogliasco' (**centre bottom**) reveals pinkish red stems, ready to release a shiny green and yellow leaf. A lone passionflower tendril (**bottom right**), which is unable to establish an anchor point, spirals into a classic example of nature's sculpture.

plants

perennials

Perennial climbers maintain a permanent presence, even in winter when they often embroider supports with a tracery of leafless stems and branches. The huge repertoire of species and cultivars provides a skeletal backbone for the climbing garden, growing in strength and impact as time passes. Many are vigorous, packing their vitality into a limited growing season and so needing firm annual pruning back to a framework of main stems. In return, they offer some of the most beautiful and floriferous displays of all plants.

Actinidia kolomikta

A vigorous, deciduous twiner, with small fragrant white flowers in summer, but noted most for its striking heart-shaped 15cm (6in) leaves, which are bright green, banded and tipped with cream and pink. This colouring is brightest in early summer and on plants growing in full sun. Train on wires, on a pergola or wall, or into a tree. 4–6m (12–20ft). Z4–8.

Akebia quinata CHOCOLATE VINE

A vigorous, semi-evergreen twining climber with a graceful, spreading habit, good for growing through trees and bushes, or on a wall, trellis or pergola. The deep green leaves, greyish beneath, each comprise five rounded leaflets. Racemes of fragrant chocolate-purple flowers appear in a mild spring, followed by long dark-purple fruits in a hot season. 9–12m (28–40ft) in a tree. Z4–9. *A. trifoliata* is similar, almost evergreen, with rich purple flowers.

Ampelopsis glandulosa var. brevipedunculata PORCELAIN BERRY

A strong, deciduous vine for large gardens, twining and climbing by tendrils. Its luxuriant mass of lobed, heart-shaped leaves, up to 15cm (6in) wide, provides good cover for walls, fences and trees. The inconspicuous flowers are followed by copious deep blue fruits after a hot summer. Plants tolerate shade but may fruit less impressively. 6m (20ft). Z5–9. *A.g.* var. *b.* 'Elegans', with pink-tinged shoots and pink and white variegated foliage, is less vigorous and suitable for confined spaces.

Aristolochia macrophylla DUTCHMAN'S PIPE

This exuberant deciduous climber with a twining habit is grown for its curious greenish-yellow and purple flowers in early summer, each like a 4cm (1½in) calabash, and for its 30cm (12in) heart-shaped leaves. It is best grown on wires on a sunny, sheltered wall or fence; in cold gardens it may die back to ground level but revives vigorously in spring. 9m (30ft). Z4–8.

Campsis radicans TRUMPET VINE

A vigorous, woody-stemmed climber scrambling up walls, fences, pergolas and over shed roofs by aerial roots. It bears deciduous leaves with 9–11-toothed 5cm (2in) leaflets and, in a sunny sheltered position, a profusion of velvety orange and red 4cm (1½in) trumpets in pendant clusters from late summer to autumn. Support plants until they are self-supporting, and prune hard in late winter to stimulate new flowering shoots. 10m (33ft). Z4–9. *C.r.* f. *flava* has rich yellow flowers. *C.* x *tagliabuana* 'Madame Galen' is very vigorous, with larger leaflets and panicles of 8cm (3in) deep apricot trumpets from late summer to autumn.

opposite left to right Although tolerant of semi-shaded positions *Actinidia kolomikta* develops its brightest leaf tints in full sun, whereas the chocolate vine, *Akebia quinata* is happy with any aspect. *Ampelopsis glandulosa* var. *brevipedunculata* 'Elegans' is a colourful luxuriant choice for larger spaces.
right The trumpet vine, *Campsis radicans*, needs plenty of space to spread itself.

Chaenomeles speciosa JAPONICA, QUINCE

A deciduous spring-flowering shrub, with tough, glossy oval leaves and thorny branching growth that is perfectly suited for training as an espalier on wall wires. Although plants are very shade-tolerant, full sun produces the most lavish display of saucer-shaped flowers, from white through to rich red, followed by large, conspicuous yellow quinces. Trained specimens should be cut back firmly after flowering. 3m (10ft). Z6–9. Good cultivars include *C.s.* **'Geisha Girl'**, a medium-sized shrub with double, deep apricot flowers; *C.s.* **'Simonii'**, a handsome, spreading dwarf variety with flattened, dark red semi-double flowers. At 1.5m (5ft), *C.* x *superba* **'Knap Hill Scarlet'** is more compact but vigorous, with brilliant orange-scarlet flowers borne profusely over a long period in spring and early summer.

Clematis

An extensive group of mainly deciduous climbers, clinging with leaf stalks and scrambling happily up shrubs, arches, tripods and pergolas. The most vigorous can be planted alone on walls and fences; others benefit from a companion such as a climbing rose. There are many kinds, from gorgeous large-flowered hybrids to dainty species, all best with their roots in cool, moist shade.

They are divided into three groups for pruning purposes:

Group 1 – early to mid-spring flowering varieties, which flower only on stems produced the previous year. These are simply trimmed tidily after flowering, to maintain size and shape.

Group 2 – early large-flowered hybrids, flowering from late spring to mid-summer

on the previous year's stems. In late winter or early spring, trim off dead growth, lightly prune good shoots to just above a pair of strong buds, and completely remove 1–2 old stems from older plants.

Group 3 – late-flowering hybrids and species, flowering from mid-summer on the current year's growth. Prune all stems hard in late winter or early spring, cutting about 30–45cm (12–18in) above ground, leaving at least 2 pairs of good buds on each stem. All those listed here are Z5–9.

Good large-flowered cultivars include:
C. **'Beauty of Worcester'**, deep violet-blue, 10cm (4in), double in early summer, single later; best in full sun. 3m (10ft) Group 2.
C. **'Belle of Woking'**, pale mauve, 10cm (4in), double, early; not a strong climber. 2–2.5m (7–8ft). Group 2. *C.* **'Comtesse de Bouchard'**, soft mauve-pink with a satin sheen, 13cm (5in), mid-summer; good in containers. 3.5m (12ft) Group 3. *C.* **'Jackmanii'**: velvety deep purple 10cm (3in) wide flowers which fade to violet, midsummer; vigorous; good for walls and latticework. 3m (10ft). Group 3. *C.* **'Lasurstern'**, mid-blue with a pale central bar, 20cm (8in), early, repeating in early autumn. 3m (10ft) Group 2. *C.* **'Marie Boisselot'** (syn. 'Mme le Coultre'), 13cm (5in) wide, pure white flowers; good in containers; deservedly popular. 5m (16ft) Group 3. *C.* **'Mrs Cholmondeley'**, a mauve-blue single, 15–20cm (6–8in), early; good for tripods. 3–5m (10–16ft) Group 2. *C.* **'Niobe'**: free-flowering throughout the summer; single, rich intense red 13cm (5in) wide flowers. 3m (10ft). Group 2. *C.* **'Perle d'Azur'**, mauve-blue rounded flowers with yellow anthers, 13cm (5in), from mid-summer. 4m (13ft); tolerant of some shade.

Group 3. **C. 'Vyvyan Pennell'**, rosy-purple fading to lilac, 20cm (8in), double in summer, single later. 3m (10ft) Group 2. **C. 'Warsaw Nike'**, rich velvety purple, 13cm (5in), mid-summer onwards; best in containers. 3m (10ft) Group 3.

Good garden clematis species include:

C. alpina

A valuable species, winter-hardy and tolerant of exposed situations. Nodding, bell-shaped 4–5cm (1½–2in) flowers with 4 tapering segments are produced in spring, ranging in colour from white, through pink and blue, with attractive fluffy seed heads later. 2–2.5m (7–8ft). Group 1. Outstanding cultivars include **C. 'Albiflora'**, creamy white; **C.a. 'Constance'**, purple-pink semi-double, free-flowering; and **C.a. 'Cyanea'**, deep blue.

C. x durandii

A non-clinging semi-herbaceous hybrid for tying in to trellis or a complementary shrub. It bears 8–10cm (3–4in) indigo–blue flowers with 4–6 tapering, slightly recurved petals. An excellent kind for containers, free-flowering all summer, and for training over shrubs such as curry plant. 2m (7ft). Group 3.

C. flammula

A charming, strongly perfumed species, laden from late summer with clusters of dozens of creamy-white 2.5cm (1in) flowers, each with 4 blunt petals. A vigorous plant for a pergola, host tree or prominent arch. 5m (16ft). Group 2.

C. macropetala

A profuse, early-flowering group, in most respects similar in appearance and per-formance to *C. alpina*, with open, bell-like flowers borne on 8cm (3in) arching stalks.

Very tough plants for exposed positions, on shrubs, arches, fences and walls. 3m (10ft) Hybrids include **C.m. 'Lagoon'**, large, deep blue; **C.m. 'Markham's Pink'**, mid-pink with purple veins. Group 1.

C. montana

All are excellent for clothing large walls or screening eyesores. Extremely vigorous, some even rampant, both species and its many hybrids are dependable late-spring climbers, most bearing 5–6cm (2–2½in) single flowers in shades of pink or white. 7–12m (22–42ft). Hybrids include **C.m. 'Freda'**, the darkest form, a deep cherry-pink; **C.m. f. grandiflora**, the largest, with 10cm (4in) pure white flowers; **C.m. 'Marjorie'**, deep salmon-pink, double; **C.m. 'Vera'**, deep pink. Group 1.

C. tangutica

Usually grown in the hybrid form **C. 'Bill**

left The thick, lemon-peel flowers and dark brown anthers of *Clematis tangutica* 'Bill Mackenzie' make an unusual display from late summer to autumn.

right Clematis seed heads can very decorative. Often starting out gleaming and silvery, they become fluffy when mature.

Mackenzie', this has nodding yellow bells, opening wide to reveal brownish anthers from late summer onwards, followed by long-lasting, silvery seed heads. Strong-growing and suitable for large pergolas. 3m (10ft) or more. Group 3.

C. texenis

A semi-herbaceous group, dying back to ground level in a hard winter, best grown in association with other shrubs and climbers as hosts, or trained on twiggy structures to make informal focal points; they are also good for containers. Their upright or nodding flowers, borne from mid-summer onwards, are typically pink or red, about 2.5cm (1in) long on 15cm (6in) stalks, with 4 fleshy segments opening outwards at their tips. 2–3m (6–10ft) Hybrids include *C.* **'Duchess of Albany'**, deep pink; *C.* **'Etoile Rose'**, rich rose-pink with a deeper central stripe; *C.* **'Gravetye Beauty'**, rich deep red. Group 3

C. viticella

This profuse-flowering late group produces nodding blooms, 4–10cm (1½–4in) across, from mid-summer, supplying valuable late colour for a trellis or large tripod in a border, and making fine companions for climbing roses. Purple shades look particularly sumptuous against pale colours or silvery foliage. 2.5–3m (8–10ft). Group 3. Hybrids include *C.* **'Etoile Violette'**, violet purple, 9cm (3½in); *C.* **'Polish Spirit'**, purple-blue with black/red anthers; *C.* **'Royal Velours'**, semi-nodding, velvety purple.

Eccremocarpus scaber CHILEAN GLORY FLOWER

Fast-growing, and evergreen except in colder climates where it dies back in winter and so is often raised from seed as an annual. Its slender, pale ferny leaves are equipped with tendrils, and it has clusters of scarlet, orange and yellow

above The characteristic, very red blooms of *Clematis texensis* are held upright like lily-flowered tulips.

right *C.* 'Beauty of Worcester' has double and semi-double flowers early in the season, followed in late summer and early autumn by these huge single blooms.

above As the satiny indigo blooms of *Clematis* x *durandii* mature, their tapering petal tips and edges reflex elegantly.

tubular flowers, 2.5cm (1in) long, throughout summer and autumn. Good trained on a tall spiral frame in a mixed border, or through shrubs and climbers. 2–3m (6–10ft). Z8–10.

Hydrangea anomala subsp. petiolaris
CLIMBING HYDRANGEA An excellent woody-stemmed climber for a shady spot, supporting itself with aerial roots. It bears coarsely toothed, heart-shaped leaves, and creamy-white and green flowers in 15cm (6in) 'lace-cap' flattened clusters in early summer. It takes several years to start flowering, and prefers shaded walls or tree trunks, with moist fertile soil. 18–25m (60–80ft), often less. Z4–9.

Jasminum officinale COMMON WHITE
JASMINE A vigorous, scrambling twiner for trees or a house wall, with supporting wires, mesh or trellis, and with some protection in cold areas. The rich green foliage is divided into 5–9 pointed leaflets, while the clusters of tubular white blooms, from early summer to early autumn, are intensely fragrant, especially on still, warm evenings. 6–9m (20–30ft). Z7–10. **J.o. f. affine** has larger, pink-tinged flowers.

J. nudiflorum WINTER JASMINE
An important winter-flowering wall shrub, with bright yellow blooms studding its bare green stems in flushes from late autumn to early spring. Excellent for covering walls and banks, and for training on pillars or pergolas, tying in the long slender stems initially to support wires. Prune hard after flowering. 3m (10ft). Z6–9.

Lonicera HONEYSUCKLE
Climbing honeysuckles are beautiful and popular scramblers and twiners, with typical spikes or clusters of open, lipped flowers, often prolific and headily fragrant. Excellent for trees, walls, pergolas, arches and tree stumps, they rapidly become major bushy features in a sunny position, with their roots ideally in moist shade.

L. japonica 'Halliana'
A vigorous evergreen honeysuckle, with soft, bright green leaves and masses of fragrant 4cm (1½in) white and yellow flowers from early summer. 6–9m (20–30ft). Z4–9. **L.j. 'Hall's Prolific'** is more profuse, flowering from an early age. The leaves of **L.j. 'Aureoreticulata'** are netted bright gold.

L. periclymenum 'Belgica' EARLY DUTCH
HONEYSUCKLE A medium-sized deciduous twiner with large, fragrant 5cm (2in) flowers, reddish-purple fading to cream, in late spring and early summer, and again in autumn. 3–4m (10–13ft). Z4–9. **L.p. 'Serotina'**, the late Dutch honeysuckle, is similar but flowers from mid-summer to autumn. ·

L. x tellmanniana

Medium-sized, this shade-loving deciduous hybrid has deep green leaves and large clusters of copper-orange 5cm (2in) flowers in early to mid-summer. 5m (16ft). Z5–9.

L. sempervirens CORAL HONEYSUCKLE

Rich green evergreen foliage and, in spring and summer, large terminal whorls of narrow 5cm (2in) trumpets, bright salmon-red with yellow interiors, make this a handsome species, best on a warm sheltered wall for the earliest flowers.

opposite left to right *Hydrangea anomala* subsp. *petiolaris* has large lace-cap flowerheads that look striking even as they fade. *Lonicera sempervirens* erupts into a summer display of colourful trumpets.
below In its autumn glory, the foliage of *Parthenocissus quinquefolia* turns almost every shade of the spectrum.

Less troubled by aphids than its more familiar relative, **L.s. 'Dropmore Scarlet'**. 4m (13ft). Z3–9.

Muehlenbeckia complexa

Something of a curiosity, this New Zealand native twines its dark, slender stems into a densely tangled, wiry curtain with a light covering of tiny, 32mm (1/8–3/4 in), round, dark green leaves. It is very useful for screening when grown on mesh or fine, horizontal wires, or for training into bushy topiary forms. Surprisingly hardy, and usually evergreen, though it prefers protection from cold winds. 6m (20ft), but to maintain fresh leaf growth, keep trimmed to within 2–3m (7–10ft) Z8–10.

Parthenocissus henryana

A graceful vine with self-clinging adhesive tendrils and ornamental leaves divided into 3–5 narrow toothed leaflets. The dark green and pinkish-bronze foliage, with silvery veins that shows well in partial shade, turns deep red in autumn. Good where its long, trailing stems can move in the breeze. 9m (30ft). Z7–9.

P. quinquefolia VIRGINIA CREEPER

This vigorous, woody-stemmed climber has dark green leaves divided into 5 oval leaflets, and brilliant crimson, scarlet and orange tints in autumn. The rampant growth can soon cover large shaded walls, trees and buildings. 15m (50ft). Z3–9.

P. tricuspidata BOSTON IVY

Vigorous and self-clinging, this vine is ideal for covering the walls of newly built houses. In mature plants, the variable leaves become large and prominently 3-lobed, rich green until they assume striking autumn tints. 20m (70ft). Z4–9. Its ornamental, equally rampant cultivar **P.t. 'Lowii'** has deeply cut, vine-like leaves with 3–7 crinkled, pointed lobes.

Rosa

Roses are classic climbing plants, conventionally divided into three cultural groups: climbers, ramblers, and species, most of the species being too vigorous for all but the largest gardens. The groups are distinguished by their different growth habit and pruning requirements.

Climbers (Cl.) generally make a few long leading stems, from which sideshoots produce large flowers, often over a long season. The sideshoots are pruned back in winter, while the leaders are fanned out in a permanent arrangement on wires or supports. These cultivars are most effective when trained on walls or pergolas.

Ramblers (R.) produce several long stems from the base each year, making a less formal, scrambling plant that is good for growing on trellis, arbours or stout pillars. They tend to have clusters of smaller flowers, growing profusely in a single main flush. Pruning consists of cutting out the oldest stems completely at the base.

This is a small selection from many cultivars; they vary dramatically in height. Generally Z7–10.

R. 'Alberic Barbier': R. Slightly fragrant, double creamy-white; mid-summer. 5m (16ft). **R. 'Albertine'**: R. Vigorous; richly scented, double coppery-pink; early summer. 5m (16ft). **R. 'Alexandre Girault'**: R. Light crimson, flattened, double; good in shade; summer. 4m (13ft). **R. 'Bobbie James'**: R. Fragrant, semi-double creamy-white; mid-summer; good in trees. 9m (30ft). **R. 'Félicité Perpétue'**: R. Fragrant, double white flowers; mid-summer; good in shade. 5m (16ft). **R. filipes 'Kiftsgate'**: Cl. Rampant; single white in clusters; mid-summer; good in trees. 12m (40ft). **R. 'Gloire de Dijon'**: Cl. Fragrant, quartered, creamy buff-apricot; repeat all summer. 4m (13ft). **R. 'Guinée'**: Cl. Fragrant, double dark red, shaded black; repeat all summer. 5m (16ft). **R. 'Madame Alfred Carrière'**: Cl. Very fragrant, double, cream tinged with pink; repeat. 5m (16ft). **R. 'Mermaid'**: Cl. Single primrose-yellow, fragrant; repeat all summer. 7m (23ft). **R. 'Phyllis Bide'**: Cl.

Small, semi-double, yellow/cream/pink/red; repeat all summer. 3m (10ft). **R. 'Souvenir du Docteur Jamain'**: Cl. Fragrant, double, deep plum; best in shade; repeat all summer. 3m (10ft). **R. 'Veilchenblau'**: R. Thornless, fragrant, semi-double lilac-blue; mid-summer. 4.5m (15ft). **R. 'William Lobb'**: Cl. Semi-double, red-purple, heavily mossed; greyish foliage; summer. 3m (10ft). **R. 'Zéphirine Drouhin'**: Cl. Thornless; fragrant, semi-double, deep cerise; repeat. 4m (13ft).

above *Rosa* 'Guinée' is a powerful climber, easily covering a large wall with its intensely fragrant velvety flowers.
opposite *Rosa* 'Félicité Perpétue' has relatively thornless stems and lustrous, almost evergreen foliage that emphasizes the clusters of creamy rosette-shaped blooms.

V. vinifera 'Purpurea' TEINTURIER GRAPE
This striking ornamental grape vine produces pale grey, downy lobed leaves that mature to a rich claret-red, turning sultry deep purple in autumn. Small greenish-black edible fruits. 7m (22ft). Z6–9. **V.v. 'Ciotat'** (syn. *V.v.* 'Apiifolia'), the parsley vine, has deeply cut ferny foliage; the greyish-green leaves of **V.v. 'Incana'**, the dusty miller grape, have white veins and downy hair like a cobweb.

Wisteria
One of the loveliest, most romantic of flowering climbers, famous for its twining habit and drooping racemes of scented pea-like flowers. It grows well on walls, but forms with long lavish racemes look best where they can drape freely, or trained as standards. Summer and winter pruning is recommended for profuse flowering.

W. floribunda JAPANESE WISTERIA
Vigorous, with attractive bright green leaves consisting of 13–19 leaflets, and slender drooping racemes of fragrant violet or bluish-purple flowers in early summer. 10m (33ft). Z5–9. **W.f. 'Alba'** is very fragrant, with white lilac-tinted flowers in 60cm (24in) racemes. **W.f. 'Multijuga'** (syn. *W.f.* 'Macrobotrys') has scented lilac flowers suffused with purple, in racemes up to 1.2m (4ft) long.

W. sinensis CHINESE WISTERIA
Extremely vigorous, a noble climber with elegant compound leaves and fragrant 2.5cm (1in) flowers, all opening together in their broad 30cm (12in) racemes, profusely in spring and sometimes again, lightly, in summer. 30m (100ft). Z5–9. **W.s. 'Alba'** is a good white; **W.s. 'Caroline'** is deep purple-blue and very fragrant; **W.s. 'Plena'** has double, rosette-shaped lilac flowers.

above *Vitis vinifera* 'Purpurea' is a strong vine and potential host for other climbers, as here for *Clematis* 'Perle d'Azur' and *C. viticella*. **opposite** An aristocrat among climbers, the Japanese wisteria, *W. floribunda* has long flower racemes that need plenty of height and space to display their extravagant size and shapeliness.

Vitis VINE
A large and versatile group of climbers with twining tendrils, many of them very vigorous and ideal for training into large trees and covering walls, pergolas, arches and fences. Many ornamental kinds assume vivid autumn tints and also produce bunches of small grapes of variable quality.

V. 'Brant'
A hybrid fruiting vine, with large, bright green 3- to 5-lobed leaves turning to brilliant shades of rusty bronze, deep red and purple in autumn, with the veins still articulated in green or yellow. The grapes are deep purple, sweet and bloomy. 9m (30ft). Z6–9.

V. coignetiae CRIMSON GLORY VINE
Rapid and vigorous growth, with young shoots covered in attractive grey down. The large, rough heart-shaped leaves, up to 30cm (12in) across turn spectacular shades of rust and crimson in autumn, especially on poorer soils. Tiny black grapes, barely edible. Spectacular for a large wall or cascading over an old tree. 25m (80ft). Z5–9.

evergreens

The foliage of evergreen climbers is capable of withstanding winter conditions unharmed; it ages, dies and falls intermittently throughout the year, rather than in a single autumn leaf-drop. Adding some of these versatile plants can enhance the winter landscape with welcome colour and interest. Despite their name, not all are green, and there are numerous tinted and variegated cultivars to transform any wall, pillar or pergola into a lively feature all year round.

Berberidopsis corallina CORAL PLANT
A semi-twining or scrambling, woody-stemmed perennial with deep green leathery leaves, oval and edged with small spines, that make an excellent backdrop for the pendent clusters of bright crimson flowers in summer and early autumn. It needs rich, lime-free soil and wires or trellis on a warm wall, with protection from strong winds or sun; in cold gardens, mulch the roots in winter. 4.5–5m (15–16ft). Z7–9.

Clematis armandii
This rampant twiner produces long, glossy dark green leaves that look handsome throughout the year. In early spring, large clusters of fragrant, creamy-white single flowers, 5cm (2in) wide, make it a romantic option for a sheltered courtyard, on a pergola or wall. 3–5m (10–16ft). Z7–9.
C.a. **'Apple Blossom'** has pink-tinted flowers and bronze young leaves, and *C.a.* **'Snowdrift'** has larger, pure white flowers.

C. cirrhosa 'Freckles'
In late autumn and early winter, this vigorous twiner produces masses of nodding 5cm (2in) bells, heavily freckled with rust red inside and pale cream on the outside. It is a handsome late-season feature for a warm wall or obelisk in mild, sheltered locations on well-drained soil, or for a conservatory. 5–6m (16–20ft). Z7–9.
C.c. **var. balearica** has sparser, ferny foliage, with 4cm (1½in) maroon-speckled flowers.

Garrya elliptica 'James Roof' SILK TASSEL BUSH This is a large, dense shrub that benefits from training on strong trellis or wires on shaded walls sheltered from cold winds. It has long leathery, wavy-edged leaves, and 20cm (8in) silver-grey male catkins suspended in profusion from mid-winter to early spring; for the rest of the year it looks rather plain, but will support bright annual climbers. 4m (13ft). Z8–9.

Hedera IVY
A familiar woody-stemmed perennial, clinging to walls and trees with adventitious roots. There is a huge range of species and cultivars, varying enormously in size, colour and habit. Most have attractive lobed or triangular juvenile leaves, and more rounded mature foliage on stout flowering stems – the small yellow-green blooms are produced in autumn, followed by black fruits in early winter. They may be trained on trellis, pergolas, tree stumps and sound walls (the searching roots and stems penetrate the smallest cracks).

H. colchica 'Dentata'
An exuberant ivy with dark green, ovate leaves 15–20cm (6–8in) long, good for covering a large sunny wall or fence. 5m (16ft). Z7–10. The leaves of **H.c. 'Dentata Variegata'** are grey-green, margined with creamy yellow, while those of **H.c. 'Sulphur Heart'** have a yellow central splash.

H. helix COMMON IVY
Extremely variable, some forms growing to 30m (100ft), with 3- to 5-lobed leaves in a wide range of tones and variegations. Most are shade-tolerant and grow happily in any soil, although the best form for moist, mild conditions is the Atlantic ivy, **H.h. 'Hibernica'**. Generally Z5–9. **H.h. 'Adam'**: A large, dense branching plant, with small, irregular greyish leaves, edged with pale cream; a good choice for low walls, ideally partnered with creamy-yellow margined **H.h. 'Eve'**. 1.2m (4ft). **H.h. 'Buttercup'**: A medium-sized form with long shoots and yellowish or pale green foliage, that needs good light but scorches in full sun. 2m (7ft). **H.h. 'Glacier'**: Dense

and short-jointed, with silver-grey leaves, narrowly edged with white; often grown as a houseplant and best sited in sheltered dappled shade. 3m (10ft). Z6–9. **H.h. 'Green Ripple'**: A bushy, fairly weak climber, with attractive, jaggedly lobed deep green leaves and light green veins. 1.2m (4ft). **H.h. 'Oro di Bogliasco'** (formerly 'Goldheart'): One of the most colourful ivies, moderately vigorous with reddish-brown stems and blue-green leaves, each sporting a bright yellow splash. 6m (20ft).

Magnolia grandiflora
A classically beautiful, very large wall shrub for a sheltered, sunny position on well-drained ground (including limy soils). It has leathery, red-felted 25cm (10in) leaves and, when several years old, creamy-white, lemon-scented flowers, 15–20cm (6–8in) wide, from mid-summer to early autumn. More than 5m (16ft). Z7–10. **M.g. 'Exmouth'** has polished, soft green leaves with reddish felt, while **M.g. 'Goliath'** has shorter, broader leaves without felt: both produce waxy cream flowers, 25cm (10in) wide, from an early age.

left Arguably the most popular variegated ivy ever introduced, *Hedera helix* 'Oro di Bogliasco' can be guaranteed to illuminate all but the shadiest of walls. Its pink immature shoots and the clear yellow and rich green of its shapely leaves produce a rich mosaic of colour. The occasional all-green shoot should be cut out at its base.
right *Solanum jasminoides* 'Album' is the prettily white form of the purple-flowered potato vine, with an airy informal habit that quickly covers a warm sheltered wall, erupting after the longest day into an effervescent display of pristine white stars in loose clusters.

Passiflora caerulea BLUE CROWN
PASSIONFLOWER Despite its exotic-looking, flowers, this rampant woody-stemmed, tendril-climber is much hardier than it looks. Although most passionflowers are frost-tender (see page 136), this is one of the few that will tolerate temperatures as low as -8°C (18°F). Its decorative lobed leaves are usually evergreen, and even if top growth gets damaged by frost, new shoots will appear in the spring. From early summer to early autumn, and especially in poor soil, it produces remarkable 8–10cm (3–4in) wide flowers, each with a prominent blue corona set against a circle of greenish-white petals. These are followed by ovoid orange fruits after a hot summer (minimum 15°C (60°F), at flowering time) in a sheltered situation. Good for wires on sunny walls, arbours, and trellis, but usually best grown on its own, as it may easily swamp other, less vigorous, climbers. It flowers best if the long stems are spurred back in spring or trained sideways. 6m (20ft) or more. Z8–10. *P.* **'Constance Elliot'** is a beautiful, slightly hardier form bearing ivory-white blooms and deep green leaves. Both are easily grown from seed.

Pyracantha 'Orange Glow'
A dense, vigorous firethorn with glossy oval leaves and massed clusters of white flowers in late spring and early summer, followed by brilliant orange-red berries through autumn and winter. If tied in to wires, it makes an excellent wall shrub for sun or shade, and may be espalier-trained or clipped into topiary shapes – trim with secateurs after flowering. In a very wet season, it may be susceptible to scab. 3.5–4m (12–13ft). Z5–9. *P.* **'Golden Charmer'** is an excellent, matching yellow partner; *P. rogersiana* **'Flava'** is another yellow-fruited form, with narrow leaves and dense growth to 3m (10ft).

Solanum crispum 'Glasnevin'
A vigorous, woody-stemmed scrambler, with bright semi-evergreen foliage and lightly fragrant, deep purple-blue flowers with a prominent central yellow beak, borne in large, loose clusters from early summer to early autumn. Plants thrive in sheltered alkaline sites in full sun or semi-shade, with their stems tied in to wires or trellis on walls or fences. 4.5–6m (15–20ft). Z8–10.

S. jasminoides 'Album' POTATO VINE
A marvellous semi-evergreen with twining leaf-stalks, quickly scrambling over large areas and covering them with its slender stems which bear small, thin leaves, glossy and bright green, and frothy masses of tiny, pure white stars with bright yellow centres. These appear from mid-summer until the first frosts, followed in a warm season by black berries. Culture is the same as for *S. crispum*, although plants need less tying in and benefit from protection in winter. 6m (20ft). Z9–11.

Trachelospermum jasminoides STAR
JASMINE A strong woody twiner, slowly climbing to 9m (30ft) if allowed. Its shiny, oval leaves, deep green and leathery, complement the slender mid-summer clusters of waxy creamy-white flowers, each 2.5cm (1in) across, with 5 curiously twisted petals and a heady fragrance. Plants prefer light, well-drained soil and a sheltered position on a warm wall or fence, or in a conservatory. Z8–10.

T. asiaticum A vigorous evergreen twiner, possibly the hardiest in its genus, it provides dense leafy cover that makes an excellent screen. It bears smaller flowers, like a creamy-white periwinkle, displayed in slim clusters during mid- and late summer. Happiest in heavy, slightly acid soil, with shelter from cold winds. 6m (20ft). Z7–10.

evergreens

above Perhaps best known of
the passionflowers is *Passiflora
caerulea,* its 10 greenish-white
tepals embellished with a halo
of blue filaments.
opposite *P.c.* 'Constance Elliot'
is a closely related form, even
more striking with its pure ivory-
white flowers.

annual and herbaceous plants

Herbaceous plants have been included with annuals as both die down completely in winter. Though playing a visual role only during the summer months, they are very useful in their ability to grow fast and flower quickly. Annuals can bring immediate interest to an area, like a new trellis or new pergola, while slower-growing perennials are still establishing themselves. They are excellent for bringing temporary interest to a seasonal display, such as a wigwam in a border. Herbaceous species bring fresh spring growth with seasonal texture and colour, adding fresh dimensions to the garden design.

Cobaea scandens CUP AND SAUCER VINE
Although usually grown as an annual, this vigorous, woody-stemmed climber is a true perennial, evergreen in mild areas and under glass. It grows fast in sunny, well-drained positions, using tendrils to fasten itself to strings or wires on pergolas, walls and trellis. In summer and autumn it produces fascinating, honey-scented 5cm (2in) bells, greenish-white at first but ripening to deep purple, backed by a green saucer. **C.s. 'Alba'** is a pure white form. 6m (20ft), more in warm climates or in a conservatory. Z8–9.

Codonopsis grey-wilsonii 'Himal Snow' (syn. *C. convolvulacea* 'Alba') A charming herbaceous perennial that revels in cool, moist soils and dappled shade, twining daintily through shrubs, netting or on pea-sticks. It bears pale green leaves, and large, pure white bells – rather like a campanula – from late summer onwards. 2.5m (8ft). Z5–6.
C. convolvulacea is similar, but with wide-open, periwinkle-blue flowers.
C. vinciflora is slightly less vigorous, with more tubular mauve-blue flowers.

Humulus lupulus 'Aureus' GOLDEN HOP
The wonderful display of deeply lobed, bright lime-green leaves makes this herbaceous perennial twiner a perfect foliage plant for screening and training on an arch, pergola or tall tripod. Growth can be rampant, however, so it is not a plant to team with climbing roses. The young spring shoots are a well-known delicacy, rather like asparagus, while in autumn, long pendent clusters of papery female cones with a resinous fragrance are produced. It is shade-tolerant but produces the best colour in full sun. 4–6m (13–20ft). Z5–8.
H. lupulus is the handsome and even more vigorous plain green species.

Ipomoea purpurea COMMON MORNING GLORY An attractive and vigorous twiner with heart-shaped leaves and 8cm (3in) trumpets in shades of blue, purple, pink, red and white, sometimes striped. Individual flowers are short-lived but produced in quick succession from mid-summer to early autumn. It is a good choice for trellis, chain link fences and for scrambling over evergreen shrubs, flowering best in a warm, sheltered site in full sun. Although a short-lived perennial, it is usually grown as an annual, often in a blend of colours. **I.p. 'Kniola's Purple-black'** is an opulent deep purple. 3m (10ft). Z5–7.
I. tricolor 'Heavenly Blue' A tender perennial for similar purposes, with huge sky-blue trumpets up to 13cm (5in) wide.

Lathyrus grandiflorus EVERLASTING PEA
A lovely magenta-pink pea with tiny fresh green leaves and a long succession (from mid-summer to mid-autumn) of 3–4cm (1½in) unscented flowers. It is good for low-level screening, in full sun or light shade, climbing on the face of shrubs, fences and netting by means of leaf-tip tendrils. 2m (7ft). Z6–9.
L. latifolius PERENNIAL PEA
A more exuberant climber up to 3m (10ft), with a number of named purple, red and pink forms, and two fine whites, **L.l. 'Albus'** and **L.l. 'White Pearl'**, which can be used, with netting, to cover dull walls and fences.

Lathyrus odoratus SWEET PEA
A favourite cottage-garden annual that uses tendrils to scramble up fences, netting, bamboo wigwams and screens. In rich moist soil, large pea flowers, often sweetly scented and long-stemmed, are produced throughout the summer; cut them frequently for vases, to ensure a good succession. Colours include pinks, purples, reds, corals, blues and whites. There are hundreds of cultivars, mostly of the large-flowered Spencer type, with ruffled petals; the recent Heavenly series, including **'Purple Nimbus'**, red **'Mars'** and lilac **'Pulsar'**, have prettily veined and marbled petals, with a picotee edge and silvery reverse. 2–3m (7–10ft). Z6–9.

Maurandya barclayana (syn. *Asarina barclayana*) A slender Mexican perennial twiner, usually grown as a tender annual, with graceful stems and soft downy leaves, and curious 8cm (3in) funnel-shaped flowers in rose-pink, deep purple or white in late summer. It prefers a fertile, leafy soil and a warm position, with wires, strings, netting or a host plant for support. 3–4m (10–13ft). Z6–9.
M. erubescens (syn. *Lophospermum erubescens*) CREEPING GLOXINIA
A tender rose-pink species, evergreen above 5°C (41°F).
M. scandens has narrower leaves and 4cm (1½in) foxglove-like flowers in red shades.

Thunbergia alata BLACK-EYED SUSAN VINE A fast-growing, twining perennial, often grown as an annual, with triangular toothed leaves and open yellow, orange or white flowers, with or without a dark purple-brown throat, from early summer until autumn. In warm, fertile soil, it makes a bright splash on a tripod in a mixed bed, or may be grown up netting or pea-sticks in a conservatory. 3m (10ft). Z7–9.

Tropaeolum majus NASTURTIUM
An annual scrambler, with succulent branching stems and large, long-stalked leaves that are shield-shaped and fresh

green ('**Out of Africa**' is a mixture with white-marbled foliage). Bright orange, yellow or red spurred flowers, up to 6cm (2½in) across, are borne from summer to autumn – both these and the peppery leaves are edible and attractive in salads. Poor soil and bright sun produce the most colourful results, on informal tripods, screens, fences or host shrubs with an open habit. It is ideal for new gardens or to fill a gap. If left to self-seed, in subsequent years it will produce strong seedlings that may be transplanted elsewhere or thinned out where they are growing. 2m (7ft). Z6–9.

T. peregrinum **CANARY CREEPER** A tender herbaceous perennial, often grown as an annual from seed. It is a valuable leaf-stalk climber for canes, fences, trees or shrubs in warm, sheltered sites, quickly providing cover while slower-growing perennials are establishing. The pale green, 5-lobed leaves and masses of irregular bright yellow flowers with fringed, erect petals are edible as well as decorative. 2–2.5m (6–8ft). Z9–10.

T. speciosum **SCOTTISH FLAME FLOWER** Masses of bright scarlet, spurred 3–4cm (1½in) flowers adorn this rhizomatous herbaceous perennial from mid-summer to autumn. It is a woodland plant, enjoying cool shade or semi-shade at the roots, with its flowers and 6-lobed leaves in full sun. The twining leaf-stalks need wires, light trellis or the twigs of an evergreen hedge like yew or box for support. In cold gardens, the roots may be overwintered in moist frost-free conditions indoors. 3m (10ft). Z7–10.

below left Sweet peas, *Lathyrus odoratus* are hard to beat as fast and easily grown annuals that excel in supplying masses of colour and fragrance, especially in cool summers.

below right *Tropaeolum speciosum*, the Scottish flame flower, is equally happy in cool conditions, with startling scarlet blooms that shine against a dark background.

tender and conservatory plants

With the benefit of a heated conservatory, or if you live in a tropical climate, it is possible to grow some wonderfully exotic climbers bringing flowers of ravishing colour and fragrance, followed by the rich texture of strange fruits. Trellis fixed to walls, tall wigwams and obelisks or simple training wires are all that is required to give them a helping hand; their own natural vigour will quickly take over.

Allamanda cathartica GOLDEN TRUMPET
A vigorous scrambler with whorls of shining evergreen leaves, leathery and lance-shaped, a fine foil for the brilliant yellow, waxy funnel-shaped flowers, 5–10cm (2–4in) across, that appear all summer and into autumn in the best form, *A.c.* 'Grandiflora'. Tie in to wires on a pillar in warm gardens or train into the conservatory roof, always in good light but with some shade at mid-summer. 5m (16ft). Minimum 13°C (55°F). *A. schottii*, the bush allamanda, is shrubbier, with deep gold flowers streaked with orange-red.

Aristolochia littoralis CALICO FLOWER
This handsome, robust evergreen twiner with large glaucous, heart-shaped leaves bears extraordinary 'Dutchman's pipe' flowers in summer. Set on long stalks, these comprise a yellowish bent tube, 2.5cm (1in) long, opening into a purple limb, marbled with white and often 10–12cm (4–5in) across. It needs a large greenhouse or conservatory, ideally in an open, airy position, perhaps by a door, as the flowers are slightly malodorous. 7m (22ft). Z9–11.

Billardiera longiflora
An interesting, slender evergreen twiner with narrow, rich green leaves and small bell-shaped flowers, greenish-yellow tinged with purple, in summer and autumn. These are followed by striking, brilliant purple-blue fleshy fruits to 2.5cm (1in) long. It grows best in well-drained soil, trained on a warm, sunny wall or host shrub, or allowed to scramble over a mound, boulder or tree stump. 'Cherry Berry' and *fructu-albo* are respectively pink- and white-fruited cultivars. 2m (7ft). Z8–11.

Bougainvillea
Brilliantly coloured clustered bracts, ranging through a vivid palette of pinks, purples and reds, coppery orange, yellow and white, make this flamboyant evergreen or semi-evergreen climber a popular conservatory choice. They are easy to grow in good light and rich warm soil, their erect thorny stems readily tied into wires or trellis on pillars and arches. 5m (16ft). Z9–11). Dozens of cultivars are available, including *B. glabra* (paper flower), rosy purple; *B.* x *buttiana* 'Mrs Helen McLean', orange; *B.* 'Dania', deep pink; *B.* 'Miss Manila', reddish pink; *B. spectabilis* 'Variegata', bright purple, leaves edged creamy-white; and *B.* Spectoperuviana Group 'Mary Palmer', pure white.

Canarina canariensis CANARY ISLAND BELLFLOWER
An herbaceous perennial scrambler, with serrated glaucous leaves and, from late autumn to spring, waxy pendulous 5cm (2in) campanula-like bells, deep orange and strongly patterned with deep red feathering. Plants need full sun, and wires or a host shrub for support. 2–3m (6–10ft). Z9–11.

Cardiospermum grandiflorum HEARTSEED
A fast-growing evergreen tendril-climber, best kept restricted to an obelisk or frame so that it does not overwhelm surrounding plants. Clusters of tiny, scented creamy-white flowers in summer are followed by 3-sided fruits up to 8cm (3in) long, green at first but ageing to

straw yellow, when they release black seeds on papery wings. 8m (28ft). Z9–11.

Cissus discolor REX BEGONIA VINE
An attractive vine often grown as a hothouse foliage plant. Its angled, red-flushed stems bear velvety lanceolate leaves, up to 15cm (6in) long and deep green, quilted and marked with a double row of pink and white blotches; their dark purplish-red reverse makes a sumptuous contrast. It is a tendril climber, needing plenty of water, humidity and light, but not hot sunshine. 3m (10ft). Z10–11.
C. antarctica, kangaroo vine, is more vigorous, with hairy woody stems and bright green toothed leaves.

Clerodendrum thomsoniae BLEEDING HEART VINE
With its conspicuous summer flowers, this bushy evergreen twiner is a good candidate for growing on a tall spiral. Striking clusters of tiny crimson flowers emerge all summer from contrasting 2.5cm (1in) white calyces, resembling a mass of miniature lanterns. It is a vigorous, woody tropical plant that needs high humidity and firm pruning. 3m (10ft). Minimum 13°C (55°F).

Clianthus puniceus LOBSTER CLAW
An evergreen or semi-evergreen shrub with long straggling stems and grey feathery leaves with 15cm (6in) leaflets arranged in pairs. From spring to early summer it produces pendulous, bright scarlet claw-like 6cm (2½in) blooms in clusters of 6–12. It is very pretty when grown on trellis for support on a pillar or wall. 5m (16ft). Z11.

opposite Most bougainvillea cultivars need plenty of space to spread their strong green stems and display their brilliant, often gaudy blooms which are in fact vivid modified leaves surrounding the true and quite insignificant tubular flowers at their centre.
right An excellent container plant for a cool conservatory, *Gloriosa superba* 'Rothschildiana' has exotic spidery blooms quite unlike any of its lily relatives.

C.p. 'Albus', creamy-white, and *C.p.* 'Roseus' (syn. 'Flamingo'), pink, are good cultivars.

Ficus pumila CREEPING FIG
Tiny heart-shaped leaves lie flat against surfaces, where the creeping stems support themselves with clinging aerial roots. It is an attractive evergreen climber for covering conservatory walls or pillars, producing an effect of a green cascade. It grows best in high humidity, with light shade from hot sun. 3m (10ft) or more. Z10–11. *F.p.* 'Minima' has very slender leaves, *F.p.* 'Variegata' is a weaker plant with white-marbled leaves.

Gloriosa superba CLIMBING LILY
A tuberous perennial, with 1–4 slender stems bearing oval leaves, tipped with tendrils. From early summer until autumn long-stalked arching flowers appear singly, opening with 6 spreading reflexed scarlet petals around a central boss of green stamens. Plants prefer light shade in summer, and need tying to canes or trellis; in late autumn they should be dried off and stored in warmth. 2–2.5m (6–8ft) Z9–11. *G.s.* 'Rothschildiana' has yellow-edged

crimson petals; *G.s.* 'Lutea' is predominantly yellow.

Hardenbergia comptoniana CORAL PEA
An appealing small twiner with evergreen 3–5 pointed leaflets and, in early summer, profuse slender clusters of tiny, soft blue or purple pea-flowers. It is best grown through a foliage climber or on a bundle of pea-sticks. 2.5–3m (8–10ft). Z10–11.
H. violacea LILAC VINE
A similar purple or lilac spring-flowering twiner; cultivars include *H.v.* 'White Crystal' and pink *H.v.* 'Rosea'.

Holboellia coriacea
A fast-growing twiner for pillars and pergolas, with evergreen leaves, each divided into 3 dark green leaflets, the central one 15cm (6in) long. Fragrant unisexual flowers appear in spring – the males small and mauve-white, the larger female blooms greenish flushed with purple – followed by 5cm (2in) fleshy sausage-shaped purple fruits. Sun and warm shelter are essential for good performance. 7m (22ft). Z9–10.

Hoya carnosa WAX PLANT
A stiffly formal twiner with aerial roots and glossy evergreen fleshy leaves, reddish when young. It is best grown on a framework that freely displays its rounded clusters of tiny, sweetly scented summer flowers, like waxy pinkish-white stars, each with a red centre and suspended drop of nectar. Shade from bright sunlight, and do not prune the flower stalks, which are perennial. 5m (16ft). Z11.
H. australis has looser trusses of fragrant white flowers with maroon markings. Shrubby *H. bella* can be grafted on *H. carnosa* to make tall standards.

Jasminum polyanthum CHINESE JASMINE
This vigorous evergreen or semi-evergreen twiner produces clusters of tiny tubular flowers, pink-flushed white and fragrant, from spring to autumn. On wires or strings, it will easily clothe a large trellis, arch, pillar or pergola, ideally in full sun although light shade is acceptable. 3m (10ft). Z10–11.

Lapageria rosea CHILEAN BELLFLOWER
Elegant, waxy, rich rose-pink or red pendent bells, 8cm (3in) long, adorn this glossy-leaved evergreen with wiry twining stems from mid-summer to autumn. It is a superb but challenging plant for well-drained soils, preferably lime-free, with shade from hot sun. Keep trained back to 5m (16ft) for the best flower production, and grow on trellis (wires are too hot in summer). 8m (28ft). Z10–11. Varieties include **'Flesh Pink'**, **'Nash Court'**, soft pink with darker marbling, and white **L.r. var. albiflora**.

Mandevilla splendens (syn. *Dipladenia splendens*) A vigorous twiner with lustrous, pale evergreen leaves, broad and pointed, and masses of tubular deep rosy-pink flowers, 10cm (4in) wide with yellow centres, from early spring to late summer. Excellent for pillars and tripods. 6m (20ft). Z9–11.

Passiflora PASSION FLOWER
Most species and cultivars of this large genus are frost-sensitive or of borderline hardiness (see page 129). They, climb by tendrils and benefit from being trained horizontally on trellis or mesh over an open space to show off their complex flowers.

P. antioquiensis BANANA PASSION FRUIT
Unusual and beautiful, with pendulous, deep rose or magenta 13cm (5in) flowers in mid-summer, followed in warm conditions by golden, banana-shaped fruit. 5m (16ft). Z9–11.

P. citrina
An unusual, slender species with delicate, yellow, star-like flowers contrasting with the dark, deeply veined, bi-lobed foliage. Perfect for training on a small frame, it will flower all year long, given bright light in a heated conservatory. 1m (3ft). Z10–12.

P. coccinea RED GRANADILLA
A vigorous species for sandy soils and warm sites, with 13cm (5in) scarlet and reddish-pink flowers with white filaments from spring to autumn. 4m (13ft). Z10-11.

P. herbertiana
Robust, almost invasive, with thin downy 3–lobed leaves and 10cm (4in) orange or greenish-yellow flowers in summer and early autumn. 6m (20ft). Z10–11.

P. incarnata MAY POPS
A vigorous N. American species with slightly glaucous leaves, sweetly scented lavender and white 8cm (3in) flowers in summer, and 5cm (2in) yellow egg-shaped fruits. 6m (20ft). Z9–11.

P. 'Incense'
Purple 12cm (5in) early summer flowers, gathered into mauve and white bands at the centre and surrounded by long, wavy filaments, are followed by edible, though acidic, fruits. 3–5m (10–16ft). Z9–11.

P. quadrangularis GIANT GRANADILLA
Rampant with angled stems and 20cm (8in) leaves, fragrant red, white and purple 8cm (3in) flowers in summer, and edible fruits up to 30cm (12in) long. 8m (28ft) Z9–11.

P. racemosa RED PASSIONFLOWER
A magnificent, medium-sized species with deeply incised leaves and drooping 30cm (12in) clusters of up to 20 brilliant scarlet flowers in mid-summer. 5m (16ft). Z10–11.

Philodendron scandens SWEETHEART VINE A useful climber for shady areas, fast-growing with fleshy stems and aerial roots for training on trellis or obelisks. With its opulent evergreen heart-shaped leaves,

15–30cm (6–12in) across, it rapidly covers lightly shaded surfaces in a warm conservatory. 4m (13ft) Z10–11.

P. erubescens BLUSHING PHILODENDRON, has even larger leaves, up to 35cm (15in) wide and tinted deep red in the cultivar **P.e. 'Imperial Red'**.

Plumbago auriculata (syn. *P. capensis*) CAPE LEADWORT Clusters of powder-blue, tubular 4cm (1¹⁄₂in) flowers and fresh pale evergreen leaves make this a perennial favourite for fertile conditions. The slender arching stems are slightly unruly, scrambling behind wires on walls and pillars, so train them carefully and prune hard after flowering and again in late winter. 4.5–6m (15–20ft). Z10–11. **P.a var. alba** is an attractive white form.

Solandra maxima GOLDEN CHALICE
A vigorous but elegant evergreen scrambler, with 15cm (6in) glossy elliptical leaves and huge 20cm (8in) tubular flowers, night-scented and deep yellow, striped inside with 5 dark purple lines. These appear in spring and summer where humidity is high (the plant is a native of tropical watersides). 6m (20ft). Z11.

plants

far left An unusual passionflower, elegant *Passiflora herbertiana* is studded all summer with slim, clear yellow flowers.
near left If given enough warmth under glass, the softly coloured blooms of *Plumbago auriculata* continue appearing well into winter.
right *Sollya heterophylla* is a delightful bushy twiner that can be raised easily from seed.

Solanum seaforthianum ITALIAN JASMINE

A twining vine, with 10cm (4in) elliptical leaves and a summer display of pendulous clusters of 2.5cm (1in) blue, purple, pink or white flowers, followed by numerous 1cm (½in) orange or scarlet berries enclosed in a papery calyx. Plants need warmth and humidity, with light shade from bright sunlight; train on wires on a conservatory wall and up onto the roof. 6m (20ft). Z10–11.

Sollya heterophylla BLUEBELL CREEPER

Numerous slender stems forming a twining mass of small evergreen foliage, glossy and narrowly oval or lance-shaped, with profuse clusters all summer of 6–12 small bell-shaped flowers in a rich shade of sky-blue. A charming plant for a trellis or tripod in a warm, lightly shaded position. 3m (10ft). Z9–11. Cultivars include white **S.h. 'Alba'**, and **S.h. 'Pink Charmer'**.

Stephanotis floribunda MADAGASCAR JASMINE

A popular evergreen twiner, with clusters of white, star-shaped tubular flowers, intensely fragrant, from spring to autumn. Its stiff stems and formal appearance make it perfect for training on spirals and obelisks, and on wires and strings into a conservatory roof. 5m (16ft). Z10–11.

Thunbergia gregorii

A perennial twiner that is often raised from seed as an annual. Its slim stems, which need tying to wires or strings on a wall or pillar, bear 8cm (3in) triangular or oval leaves on winged stalks, and summer crops of rich, orange tubular flowers, 5cm (2in) across with spreading lobes. 3m (10ft). Z10–11.

vegetables and fruit

Whether you have space for a small potager or a full-scale kitchen garden, the benefits of having freshly picked fruit or vegetables can be combined with the decorative potential of many tall productive plants that are natural climbers or lend themselves to vertical training. Training fruits as fans, espaliers or cordons on wires, walls and fences or simply planting some bean seeds around a wigwam makes maximum use of a limited space, supplying decorative accents and adding height to their surroundings.

Actinidia deliciosa KIWI FRUIT, CHINESE GOOSEBERRY A vigorous twining climber with shoots densely covered with attractive reddish hairs and huge, heart-shaped leaves. Edible, hairy-skinned, green-fleshed fruits follow fragrant cream or buff-yellow flowers. A male should be planted to fertilize every 5–6 females, or grow a self-fertile cultivar; successful fruiting only occurs on mature plants on a sunny pergola, warm wall or on strong supports under glass in cooler gardens. Prune hard in winter, and summer prune new growth just beyond setting fruit. 9m (30ft). Z7–10. Female cultivars include **'Abbot'** and **'Hayward'**, best pollinated by male **'Tomuri'**; **'Blake'** and **'Jenny'** are self-fertile.

Cydonia oblonga EDIBLE QUINCE
Handsome deciduous tree, full of character, with branches that can be trained as a fan or palmette on a warm wall. Pink or white 5cm (2in) flowers appear in spring, followed by large apple- or pear-shaped fruit, downy, very fragrant and rich yellow when mature in mid-autumn; store away from other fruit. Pruning consists of thinning crowded branches in winter, and summer pruning sideshoots of trained forms to 2–3 leaves. 4–6m (13–20ft). Z4–9. Recommended cultivars include **'Champion'**, apple-shaped, **'Meech's Prolific'**, pear-shaped and slow-growing, **'Vranja'** (syn. 'Bereczki'), large pear-shaped (all self-fertile).

Malus domestica APPLE
Apples on dwarfing rootstocks are easily grown as espaliers or cordons on posts and wires in a cool, airy position, or on fences (house walls can be too warm), and their flexible branches may be shaped into quite complex forms that are both ornamental and productive. Trained apples should be chosen from spur-bearing cultivars, not tip-bearing kinds, which cannot be closely pruned to shape. Prune established trees in late summer; shorten new shoots to 5 leaves, and shoots growing from existing spurs to 2 leaves. 3–9m (10–30ft) according to rootstock. Z5–9. There are hundreds of cultivars, including (in order of ripening) **'Discovery'**, **'George Cave'**, **'Early Victoria'** (culinary), **'James Grieve'**, **'Spartan'**, **'Egremont Russet'**, **'Sunset'**.

Prunus armeniaca APRICOT
A gourmet fruit that needs cold winters, warm springs and long, sunny summers to crop well. An elegant tree, with beautiful 4cm (1½in) pink or white flowers in very early spring and ripe fruit by mid-summer. It is best on a warm sheltered wall or under glass, with the blossom hand-pollinated in a cold season. Easily trained as a large fan on canes or wires, spur-prune by pinching back sideshoots to 8cm (3in) in early summer. Thin fruits to 10cm (4in) apart. 10m (33ft), but less if trained. Z5–9. Good cultivars (all self-fertile) include **'Alfred'**, **'Moor Park'** and **'New Large Early'**.

Prunus avium Hybrids SWEET CHERRY
Even on semi-dwarfing rootstocks, a cherry will make a very large tree and a trained fan can spread to 6m (20ft) high and wide. Grow on a warm wall, sheltered from cold winds and late frosts, and protected from birds, in a position where the spectacular blossom can be seen, together with the fiery autumn leaf tints. Pinch back sideshoots on mature fans to 6 leaves in mid-summer, and further shorten these to 4 buds in early autumn. 20m (70ft), but less

when trained. Z3–9. Most varieties need to be cross-pollinated, but **'Stella'**, **'Compact Stella'**, **'Lapins'** (syn. 'Cherokee') and **'Sunburst'** are self-fertile.

Prunus cerasus Hybrids ACID CHERRY
Very similar to the sweet cherry, except that birds are less of a problem, and routine pruning differs, because acid cherries fruit on new stems, rather than on permanent spurs. Prune by cutting out overcrowded and very old stems each year after fruiting, and tie in new replacement shoots as they grow. 6m (20ft). Z3–9. Cultivars are self-fertile, the best known being **'Morello'**.

Prunus domestica PLUM, GAGE, DAMSON
Vigorous, spreading tree (even on semi-dwarfing rootstocks) for training as a fan on wires on a large, sunny wall, which improves flowering and fruiting, especially where spring frosts are a problem. Prune in mid-summer by pinching back all sideshoots to 15cm (6in), and again after fruiting to 8cm (3in). 12m (42ft), much less when trained. Z5–9. Many fine-flavoured varieties need another compatible kind nearby for fertilization – in smaller gardens, grow a self-fertile kind such as **'Victoria'** plum, **'Denniston's Superb'** or **'Reine Claude de Bavay'** gages, and **'Merryweather'** damson.

Pyrus communis PEAR
Pears are similar to apples in cultural needs, although they will tolerate more heat, so benefit from being trained on a house wall, and, with less pliable stems, need early tying in to wires when trained as espaliers, cordons and fans. Their blossom is supreme, smothering the branches in a white froth in spring. Owing to a limited choice of rootstocks, growth can be quite vigorous, and firm pruning (in the same way as for apples) is necessary. 6m (20ft). Z4–9. Cultivars need a compatible partner for cross-pollination, and are usually divided into 3 groups according to flowering time. Choice cultivars include **'Beurré Hardy'**, **'Concorde'**, **'Conference'**, **'Doyenné du Comice'** and **'Joséphine de Malines'**.

Ribes rubrum RED AND WHITE CURRANT

Easily grown in both sun and shade, cropping lavishly at slightly different seasons according to aspect, red currants are easily trained against a wall or fence as fans or single and multiple cordons, and also crop well in the open, trained on posts and wires. They fruit mid- to late summer, and usually need netting against birds and squirrels. Summer prune trained forms by cutting sideshoots back to 5 leaves in mid-summer (this helps expose fruit to maximum light),

below left Spur-bearing apples – varieties that produce fruits on stubby sideshoots pruned close to the main stems – are ideal for training on supports such as fences, posts and wires, or as here, metal arches.
below right Many brambles can be trained in the same way, especially species such as *Rubus phoenicolasius* that combine fruitfulness with beauty.

and further shorten them to 4cm (1½in) after leaf-fall. 2m (7ft) Z6–9. Cultivars (self-fertile) include **'Jonkheer van Tets'**, **'Red Lake'** and **'Stanza'**. The white currant is a colour variant, *R. rubrum* (White Currant Group), and treated in the same way: good cultivars are **'White Grape'** and **'Versailles Blanche'** (syn. 'White Versailles').

Ribes uva-crispa GOOSEBERRY

These generally prickly fruits are much easier to harvest and prune if trained as fans or cordons on walls, fences or posts and wires, and also produce finer quality green, yellow, white or red berries in restricted forms. Cultivation and pruning are the same as for red currants. 1.5–2m (5–7ft) Z5–8. Cultivars (self-fertile) include **'Careless'**, green; **'Leveller'**, yellow; **'Whinham's Industry'**, red; **'Whitesmith'**, greenish-white; and mildew-resistant **'Invicta'** (green) and **'Pax'** (red).

Rubus fruticosus BLACKBERRY

Long flexible canes make this a suitable subject for training as espaliers and fans, either free-standing on posts and wires, or on a warm house wall, but they are also good for arches and arbours, especially if a thornless variety is chosen. They need feeding lavishly, and annual pruning after cropping, when the fruited canes are cut out and replaced by the new stems, which fruit the following season. 8m (28ft) Z6–9. Good varieties include **'Black Satin'**, **'Loch Ness'** (thornless), **'Oregon Thornless'**, **'Parsley Leaved'** and **'Waldo'** (thornless.). Close relatives with similar needs and uses include *Rubus* (Loganberry Group), especially the thornless loganberry LY654, and decorative *R. phoenicolasius* or (Japanese) wineberry, with handsome red, bristly foliage and conical cherry-red fruits.

above Grape vines, *Vitis vinifera*, are supreme climbers both outdoors and under glass, if they are tightly pruned and trained, and tied in on a lattice of productive stems.

Rubus idaeus RASPBERRY

Raspberries have an upright habit and are usually tied along horizontal wires in a free-standing row, making a useful live fence or screen. Plants are sometimes trained as a V-shaped row, with two sets of wires secured to a triangular frame at each end – the current fruiting canes are tied to one side, while their young replacements are tied to the other side, so avoiding confusion at picking time. Summer-fruiting cultivars are pruned after harvest, cutting out the exhausted canes for replacement by the current year's new canes; autumn-fruiting cultivars are cut to the ground in late winter. 1.5m (5ft). Z3–8. Summer cultivars include

'Malling Promise', 'Glen Clova', 'Malling Jewel'; autumn kinds are 'Leo', 'Autumn Bliss' and 'Heritage'.

Vitis vinifera GRAPE VINE

An important fruit crop, easily grown in gardens if the pliant vines are trained on wires on a wall, pergola, arch or arbour, adding a hint of romance and luxury when laden with fruit. Full sun is essential, together with a sunny frost-free position (under glass in cold areas and for certain cultivars), efficient training to admit maximum sunlight and air, and careful pruning during the season to prevent excess leaf growth at the expense of fruit. Once a framework of rods is trained and tied in, prune after flowering, cutting sideshoots 2 leaves beyond a fruit-truss; subsequent sideshoots are stopped after one leaf. After harvest the exhausted shoot is cut back to 2 buds. 15m (50ft), much less when trained. Z6–9. There are many cultivars of different colours and qualities – whether for wine or dessert, outside or for indoor cultivation according to locality. Good choices include (indoor black) 'Black Hamburg', 'Black Prince', 'Lady Hastings', 'Madresfield Court'; (indoor white) 'Buckland Sweetwater', 'Chasselas Vibert', 'Foster's Seedling', 'Royal Muscadine'; (outdoor black) 'Leon Millot', 'New York Muscat', 'Pirovano 14', 'Triumph d'Alsace'; (outdoor white) 'Himrod Seedless', 'Oliver Irsay', 'Perle de Czaba', 'Siegerrebe'.

climbing vegetables from seed

Peas and beans with their lush foliage and coloured flowers and pods are ornamental stars of the vegetable garden, creating fast-growing features both there and in flower beds and borders. They may be trained on wigwams, tripods or cylinders of netting, over arches where their beans can dangle teasingly, and even on rows of canes to make productive seasonal screens and temporary windbreaks.

Cucurbita maxima, C. moschata, and C. pepo WINTER SQUASH

Dependable, often rampant annual vines with conspicuous cream, yellow, orange, even black fruits of varied shape. They climb with tendrils and sprawling hairy stems that may be tied to strings and wires on strong supports such as a trellis, obelisk, arch or pergola in a sunny sheltered position. The long trailing shoots may need light pruning to keep plants tidy. Cultivars with smaller fruits are best for vertical and overhead training. Sow or plant them after the last spring frosts, and gather the fruits in autumn for maturing in sun for a few days, before storing for winter. 4m (13ft) or more. Z9–11. There are many cultivars, including 'Blue Kuri', 'Butternut Waltham', 'Delicata', 'Golden Cushaw', 'Large Cheese', 'Sweet Dumpling', 'Turk's Turban', 'Uchiki Kuri'.

Lablab purpureus (syn. Dolichos lablab) HYACINTH BEAN

A rampant twining bean with large, purple-tinted foliage and 40cm (16in) spikes of deep mauve pea flowers in late summer, followed by edible maroon pods, 15 x 5cm (6 x 2in). Adds an exotic, tropical flourish to arches, pergolas and similar larger structures. Sow or plant after the last spring frosts, in a warm sunny position or under glass. 6m (20ft). Z9–11

Lagenaria siceraria BOTTLE GOURD

An example of a large number of species of ornamental gourd, grown for their bizarre shapes and complex colours. A vigorous annual vine, climbing by means of tendrils, with large rough leaves, conspicuous 13cm (5in) yellow flowers and narrow, cream-splashed green fruit, up to 2m (7ft) long, often shorter with bulbous necks. They are lush, spectacular features when trained on strong arches and pergolas where the fruits can hang freely. Sow or plant after the last spring frosts, and grow in a warm sheltered place. 9m (30ft). Z9–11. Other varieties include blue-grey 'Twonga', and long, white-spotted 'Amphore'.

Lycopersicon esculentum TOMATO

A sun-loving perennial, usually grown as an annual, that scrambles weedily in the wild, but in gardens tall ('indeterminate') cultivars can be trained as cordons on upright canes, or tied to wigwams or trellis to create edible focal points. Plants are normally kept to a single main stem, although some sideshoots can be retained to create a decorative fan or espalier on a wall or fence; under glass, many small-fruited cultivars are readily trained high into the roof as summer climbers, their trusses of red, gold or yellow fruits suspended freely below the vines. Sow or plant outdoors after the last spring frosts, a month or more earlier for growing under cover. 2m (6ft). Z9–11. The enormous range of up-to-date and heritage cultivars includes **'Andine Cornue'**, **'Banana Legs'**, **'Gardener's Delight'**, **'Santa'**, **'Striped Cavern'**, **'Sungold'**, **'Tigerella'**, **'Yellow Brandywine'**.

Phaseolus coccineus RUNNER BEAN

A vigorous twining bean, akin to the pole bean and valuable for similar situations, although its heavy canopy of foliage requires stronger supports. Excellent for summer cover on an arbour, mingling with hops, clematis or nasturtiums. The flowers are classically bright scarlet, occasionally pink, white or bicoloured. A tender perennial, usually sown or planted as an annual after the last spring frosts; harvest regularly for a long season. 4–5m (13–16ft) Z9–11. Good cultivars include **'Achievem'**, **'Desiree'**, **'Enorma'**, **'Painted Lady'**, **'Red Knight'**, **'Scarlet Emperor'**, **'Sunset'**.

Phaseolus vulgaris POLE BEAN, CLIMBING FRENCH BEAN

This is a huge race of legumes with white, pink or mauve flowers and long flat or rounded pods that may be green, gold or purple, sometimes with extravagant speckles and stripes. Climbing varieties are productive and can be used for the same roles as *Lablab purpureus*. Sow or plant after the last spring frosts, in a warm sunny position, and harvest regularly to sustain long cropping. 4m (13ft). Z9–11. Choice cultivars include **'Climbing Blue Lake'**, **'Borlotto'**, **'Burro d'Ingegnoli'**, **'Corona d'Oro'**, **'Hunter'**, **'Kentucky Blue'**, **'Kingston Gold'**, **'Or du Rhin'** (syn. 'Marvel of Venice'), **'Purple Podded Climbing'**, **'Rob Roy'**, **'Viola Cornetti'**.

Pisum sativum PEA

Climbing peas are more productive than dwarf kinds, and, with their white, pink or mauve flowers and green or purple pods, make handsome seasonal pillars or tripods as finials at the corners of beds. They climb by means of tendrils, and need strings or netting for support. Sow in succession from early spring until early summer, and pick regularly for a continuous supply. 1.5–2m (5–7ft). Z7–10. The limited number of cultivars includes **'Alderman'**, **'Purple Podded'**, and mauve-flowered mangetout **'Carouby de Maussane'**.

below left Ornamental gourd mixtures often include this pretty gold and green bicolored form, which is edible if picked while young.
below centre Runner beans were first grown in Europe as ornamental climbers, ideal for creating summer screens of scarlet flowers.
below right Mangetout peas are productive climbers, with high yields of crisp, juicy edible pods for summer harvest.

index

Page numbers in *italic* refer to captions

PLANT HARDINESS ZONES

The zones given for each plant represent the range in which the plant may be successfully grown. The zone ratings are those devised by the United States Department of Agriculture. The chart below indicates the average annual minimum temperature of each zone. Zoning data can only give rough guidelines. Plant hardiness depends on a great many factors, and within any one zone particular regions may be endowed with more or less favourable conditions. In particular it should be noted that the upper limit hardly applies in western Europe, where summers are not as hot as those in North America; so, for example, most plants coded Z4–7 will grow happily in western European zones 8 and 9.

CELSIUS	ZONES	°FAHRENHEIT
below -45	1	below -50
-45 to -40	2	-50 to -40
-40 to -34	3	-40 to -30
-34 to -29	4	-30 to -20
-29 to -23	5	-20 to -10
-23 to -18	6	-10 to 0
-18 to -12	7	0 to 10
-12 to -7	8	10 to 20
-7 to -1	9	20 to 30
-1 to 4	10	30 to 40
above 4	11	above 40

AUTHOR'S ACKNOWLEDGMENTS

I would like to thank the many people who gave their time and skill in the making of this book, especially Steven Wooster for his care and expertise in producing the most ravishing photographs. Special thanks go to those who contributed to the step by step projects: Rosie Brister for unstinting effort and creativity under the hottest sun to produce the gorgeous rustic gazebo, Lloyd Christie Garden Architecture for designing the elegant wooden obelisk, and Ben May for his generosity and skill in creating the beautiful living arbour. And I am very grateful to Trisha and Walter Böetchi, Mary and Nigel Chapman at Hode Pottery, Mrs Sarah Craven and Gill Webb for their liberal hospitality and for allowing us to use their gardens for photographic locations. **Joan Clifton**

All Avant Garden products designed by Joan Clifton (featured in this book on pages 1, 71, 77, 89, 92, 93 and 94/95), are obtainable by mail order worldwide. Joan Clifton can be contacted through Avant Garden at www.avantgarden.co.uk (email info@avantgarden.co.uk), and through her design consultancy www.horticouture.com

PUBLISHER'S ACKNOWLEDGMENTS

The Publisher would like to thank the following people for their invaluable help in producing this book: Andi Clevely, David Joyce and Sarah Mitchell.

PHOTOGRAPHIC ACKNOWLEDGMENTS

a=above *b*=below *l*=left *r*=right *c*=centre *d*=designer

Jean-Pierre Gabriel 72–3 (Ost/Schoten); 84–5
Garden Picture Library/Ron Sutherland 90*l* (d: Anthony Paul)
Jerry Harpur 26–7 (Bill Overholt, d: Chittock, Seattle); 42–3 (David Pearson, Constructor: Brian Berry, London); 66–7 (d: Iris Kaplow, New York); 67*r* (d: Michael Balston, Wiltshire); 74 (d: Sonny Garcia, San Francisco); 78–9 (d: Oehme & van Sweden, Washington DC); 96–7 (Lord and Lady Tollemache, Helmingham Hall, Suffolk); 99 (d: Rosemary Verey and Rupert Goldby at The Old Rectory, Sudborough, Northamptonshire)
Andrew Lawson 6–7 (David Wheeler & Simon Dorrell); 16 (d: Anthea Gibson); 56; 82*b* (The Old Rectory, Sudborough, Northamptonshire); 83*a* (d: Kristina Fitzsimmons); 98 (d: Arne Maynard); 125 © FLL; 126 © FLL
Courtesy of **Lloyd Christie** 69
Ray Main/Mainstream 68 (d: Tindale Batstone Landscape Design)
Marianne Majerus 22–3 (d: David French), 29 © FLL; 54–5 (d: Susan Campbell); 62–3 (d: Paul Cooper); 90*r* © FLL
Michael Paul 75*br*
Gary Rogers 18–9 (Landcraft Environments Ltd, New York); 28; 30–1 (d: Ursula & Klaas Schnitzke-Spijker, Germany)
Steven Wooster 1; 2 and 3 (Wyken Hall, Suffolk); 4; 5; 8–9; 10 (Roseraie de l'Hay-les-Roses, France); 12; 13 (Waimarino, NZ); 14*a*; 14*b* (Josie Martin, Akaroa, NZ); 15*a* (The Old Vicarage, Norfolk); 15*b* (d: Bowles & Wyer, London); 17 (Les Jardins du Prieuré Notre Dame d'Orsan, France); 19*r* (Wilsons Mill, NZ); 20*l* (Ann Mollow, London); 20–1 (Saling Hall, Essex); 21*r* (The Gardens of Gaia, Sissinghurst, Kent); 24–5 (Wyken Hall, Suffolk); 26; 32 (d: Peter Styles, Chelsea Flower Show 1998); 33*ar* (The Old Vicarage, Norfolk); 33*al* (d: Bowles & Wyer, London); 33*br* (Joan Clifton, London); 33*bl* (d: Bowles & Wyer, London); 34*l*; 35–37; 38*l* (O'Sullivan Stables Garden, Mata Mata, NZ); 38–9 (d: Bowles & Wyer, London); 40 (La Coquetterie, France, d: Pascal Cribier); 41 (Les Jardins du Prieuré Notre Dame d'Orsan, France); 44–5 (Monet's Garden, Giverny); 46 (Barbara Lee Taylor, Akaroa, NZ); 47*l* & *c*; 47*r* (Monet's Garden, Giverny); 48*a* (Lea Dunster, Akaroa, NZ); 48*b* and 49*a* (Ayrlies, NZ); 49*b* (Briar Rose Cottage, NZ); 50 and 51 (Les Jardins du Prieuré Notre Dame d'Orsan, France); 52 and 53*ar* (The Old Rectory, Sudborough, Northhamptonshire); 53*al* (Mien Ruys, Holland); 53*br* (The Old Vicarage, Norfolk); 53*bl* (Suzette Gardens, Rakaia, NZ); 57 (Burford House Gardens, Shropshire); 63*r*; 64 (d: Anthony Paul); 65 (d: Eiji Morozumi); 70; 71; 75 (all Chaumont 9th International Garden Festival) *ar* ('The Observatory' d: Philip Brown and Martin Lonsdale, UK), *al* ('Code Naturel', d: P & P, Berlin), *bl* ('Mente la Menta', d: Marco Antonini, Gianna Attiani, Roberto Capecci, Maria Elisabetha Cattaruzze, Daniela Mongini & Rafaella Sini, Italy); 76; 77; 79*r*; 80–1 (Saddlecombe, Kent); 82*a* (d: Anthony Paul); 83*b* (Nellie Hijman, Holland); 86*a* (Hampton Court Palace Flower Show 1999, d: Susanna Brown); 86*b* and 87*a* (Nellie Hijman, Holland); 87*b*; 88–9 (Piet Oudolf, Holland); 89*a* and *c* (De Brinkhof, Holland); 89*b* (d: Avant Garden); 92; 93*ar*; 93*ac*; 93*al*; 93*br*; 93*bl*; 93*bc* ('Garden Architecture', London); 97*r* and 100 (The Organic Centre, Ireland); 101 (Cartier Garden, Chelsea Flower Show 1998); 102*a* (Bourton House, Gloucestershire); 102*b* (Hatton Gardens, Kent); 103 (Wyken Hall, Suffolk); 104–105; 106, 107*ar* and *br* (Les Jardins du Prieuré Notre Dame d'Orsan, France); 107*al* (Yalding Organic Gardens, Kent); 107*bl* (The Organic Centre, Ireland), 108-111; 112–113 (Monet's Garden, Giverny); 114 (Les Jardins du Prieuré Notre Dame d'Orsan, France); 115*ar* (The Plantsman Nursery, Devon); 115*al* (Andrew Kearny, London); 115*br* (Yalding Organic Garden, Kent); 115*bl* (The Beth Chatto Garden, Essex); 116–123; 124 (Broughton Castle, Oxfordshire);127; 128; 129-131 (Joan Clifton, London); 133*r* (Mt Stewart, County Down, Northern Ireland); 133*l*; 134 (The Chapple's Garden Auckland, NZ); 135 (The Plantsman Nursery, Devon); 136*r*; 136*l* & 137 (The Plantsman Nursery, Devon); 139*r* (De Brinkhof, Holland); 139*l*; 140; 141*r* and *c*; 141*l* (The Old Vicarage, Norfolk); 144 (Burford House, Shropshire)
Yayoi 94; 95